HANDY HINTS

A Family Handyman Book

Hardcover ISBN: 978-1-62145-917-0
Paperback ISBN: 978-1-62145-922-4
E-pub ISBN: 978-1-62145-923-1
Component number: 119100110H

We are committed to both the quality of our products and the service we provide
to our customers. We value your comments, so please feel free to contact us at
TMBBookTeam@TrustedMediaBrands.com.

Text, photography and illustrations for *Family Handyman Handy Hints* are
based on articles previously published in *Family Handyman* magazine
(familyhandyman.com).

PHOTOGRAPHY AND ILLUSTRATION CREDITS
32 Frank Rohrbach III; **100** GE Appliances; **130** *bl* Maytag; **131** *tr* HealthCraft Products
Inc.; **132** *t* promenaid.com
Getty Images: Chapter openers/hexagon pattern carduus; **92** Monty Rakusen; **100,
101** BanksPhotos; **105** Jeffrey Coolidge; **130** *tl* breckeni; **130** *tr* Jon Lovette; **132** *br*
Rosley Majid; **133** *tl* William Geddes; **133** *tr* kievith
Shutterstock: 17 Monkey Business I; **20** Patrycja Grobelny; **76** Himchenko.E; **80** united
photo studio; **115** BonD80; **198** fotosen55

All other photographs by Trusted Media Brands staff photographers

A NOTE TO OUR READERS
All do-it-yourself activities involve a degree of risk. Skills, materials, tools and site
conditions vary widely. Although the editors have made every effort to ensure
accuracy, the reader remains responsible for the selection and use of tools, materials
and methods. Always obey local codes and laws, follow manufacturer instructions
and observe safety precautions.

PRINTED IN CHINA
1 3 5 7 9 10 8 6 4 2

SAFETY FIRST—ALWAYS!

Tackling home improvement projects and repairs can be endlessly rewarding. But as most of us know, with the rewards come risks. DIYers use chain saws, climb ladders and tear into walls that can contain big and hazardous surprises.

The good news is, armed with the right knowledge, tools and procedures, homeowners can minimize risk. As you go about your projects and repairs, stay alert for these hazards:

ALUMINUM WIRING
Aluminum wiring, installed in millions of homes between 1965 and 1973, requires special techniques and materials to make safe connections. This wiring is dull gray, not the dull orange characteristic of copper. Hire a licensed electrician certified to work with it. For more information, go to *cpsc.gov* and search for "aluminum wiring."

SPONTANEOUS COMBUSTION
Rags saturated with oil finishes like Danish oil and linseed oil, and oil-based paints and stains can spontaneously combust if left bunched up. Always dry them outdoors, spread out loosely. When the oil has thoroughly dried, you can safely throw them in the trash.

VISION AND HEARING PROTECTION
You should wear safety glasses or goggles whenever working on DIY projects that involve chemicals, dust and anything that could shatter or chip off and hit your eye. Sounds louder than 80 decibels (dB) are considered potentially dangerous. Sound levels from a lawn mower can be 90 dB, and shop tools and chain saws can be 90 to 100 dB.

LEAD PAINT
If your home was built before 1979, it may contain lead paint, which is a serious health hazard, especially for children age 6 and under. Take precautions when you scrape or remove it. Contact your public health department for detailed safety information or call 800-424-LEAD (5323) to receive an information pamphlet. Or visit *epa.gov/lead*.

BURIED UTILITIES
A few days before you dig in your yard, have your underground water, gas and electrical lines marked. Just call 811 or go to call811.com.

SMOKE AND CARBON MONOXIDE (CO) ALARMS
The risk of dying in reported home structure fires is cut in half in homes with working smoke alarms. Test your smoke alarms every month, replace batteries as necessary and replace units that are more than 10 years old. As you make your home more energy-efficient and airtight, existing ducts and chimneys can't always successfully vent combustion gases, including potentially deadly carbon monoxide (CO). Install a UL-listed CO detector, and test your CO and smoke alarms at the same time.

FIVE-GALLON BUCKETS AND WINDOW COVERING CORDS
Anywhere from 10 to 40 children a year drown in 5-gallon buckets, according to the U.S. Consumer Products Safety Commission. Always store them upside-down and store those containing liquid with the covers securely snapped.

According to Parents for Window Blind Safety, hundreds of children in the United States are injured every year after becoming entangled in looped window treatment cords. For more information, visit *pfwbs.org*.

WORKING UP HIGH
If you have to get up on your roof to do a repair or installation, always install roof brackets and wear a roof harness.

ASBESTOS
Texture sprayed on ceilings before 1978, adhesives and tiles for vinyl and asphalt floors before 1980, and vermiculite insulation (with gray granules) all may contain asbestos. Other building materials made between 1940 and 1980 could also contain asbestos. If you suspect that materials you're removing or working around contain asbestos, contact your health department or visit *epa.gov/asbestos* for information.

CONTENTS

CHAPTER 1

CLEANING

POWER SCOUR

With an inexpensive electric toothbrush, you can add a modern twist to routine cleaning. Rapid vibration of the brush head will quickly scrub out stubborn dirt without all the elbow grease, while the long handle can get the brush into hard-to-reach places.

Bag the Dust

Minimize the mess when you're cutting or drilling a hole in drywall. Tape a bag below the work zone to catch the dust. Use an easy-release tape to avoid wall damage.

Dust Catcher

When you need to make small repairs on wall surfaces, place wide painters tape just below the area and fold it back to catch the dust. It saves on cleanup and helps limit the airborne dust.

No-Smell Gym Bag

A gym bag can get stinky after a while, but here's an easy way to prevent that: Put silica gel cat litter in a small square of fabric and close it with a zip tie. The crystals absorb odor-creating moisture, keeping your bag fresh. Replace the crystals monthly or as needed.

Silica gel crystals in a bag

Plastic
bag

WINDOW TREATMENT PROTECTION

When prepping for painting, taking down Roman shades and blinds
and putting them back up again can be time-consuming. Instead,
leave them in place, wrap them in plastic bags and paint around them.

BLAST SCREENS CLEAN

If you have an air compressor and an air nozzle, you can clean window and door screens in seconds without removing them. Just turn the pressure to 60 psi and blow away any dust, debris and cobwebs.

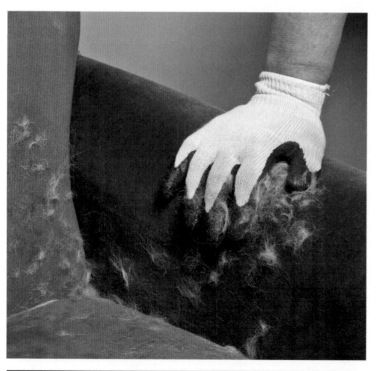

PET HAIR REMOVER

Nonslip rubber-dipped gloves that you can purchase at home centers and hardware stores are perfect for removing pet hair from upholstered furniture. Simply run your gloved hand over the surface of the fabric. The hair will roll up into a bunch, leaving the upholstery virtually lint-free.

Clean Jars with BBs

Antique jars and bottles can be really hard to get clean. To remove tough stains, put a little soapy water in the bottle and add a few tablespoons of BBs. After a bit of soaking and several shakes, the bottles should come clean. You can also use the same method to clean peanut butter and jam jars. If you rinse and dry the BBs afterward, you can reuse them. Just remember to keep them out of the sink and drain, and away from small children and pets.

Air Duct Covers

When you're creating dust during a home improvement project, cover the air supply and return air ducts with plastic and seal the edges with tape. Dust sucked into return air ducts can plug your furnace filter, and small particles can pass through the filter and coat the house with fine dust when the blower turns on. Dust that settles inside air supply ducts will come blasting out when your system starts up. Closing the damper on a supply register helps but doesn't seal it completely. Just be sure to turn off the heating/cooling system while the ducts are covered. Operating the system with restricted airflow can damage it.

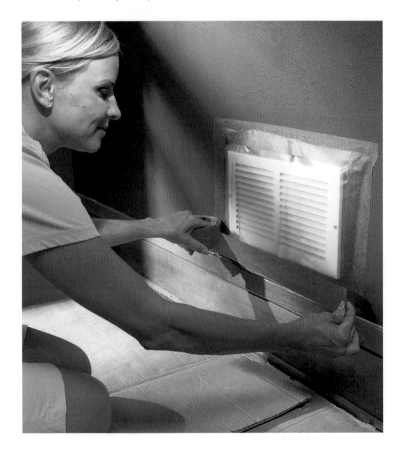

DUST WITH YOUR DRYER

Blankets, pillows, slipcovers, drapes and other textiles not only trap household dust, but they also create it as they shed and disintegrate. Curtains and drapes in particular get very dusty because they absorb moisture and dirt from the outside and act as a landing pad for dust from ceiling fans and air vents. The best idea is to buy machine-washable items and launder them once or twice a year. For non-machine-washable textiles, throw them in the dryer on the air-fluff setting (with no heat) for 20 minutes with a damp towel. The towel will attract pet hair, and the tumbling movement and airflow will remove the smaller particles for you.

Damp towel

EASIER GROUT HAZE CLEANUP

The thousands of microscopic fabric hooks on a microfiber cloth make it perfect to cut through the dried grout haze left after a tiling project. You'll still have to rinse and repeat, but the haze will clean up faster than it would with an ordinary rag.

Wash Your Shower Curtain

Toss your grimy shower curtain or liner in the washing machine instead of the garbage and save a trip to the store and a few bucks. Add about a quarter cup of vinegar to a warm-water wash cycle and your shower curtain will come out fresh and clean. The vinegar also helps to kill mold and mildew.

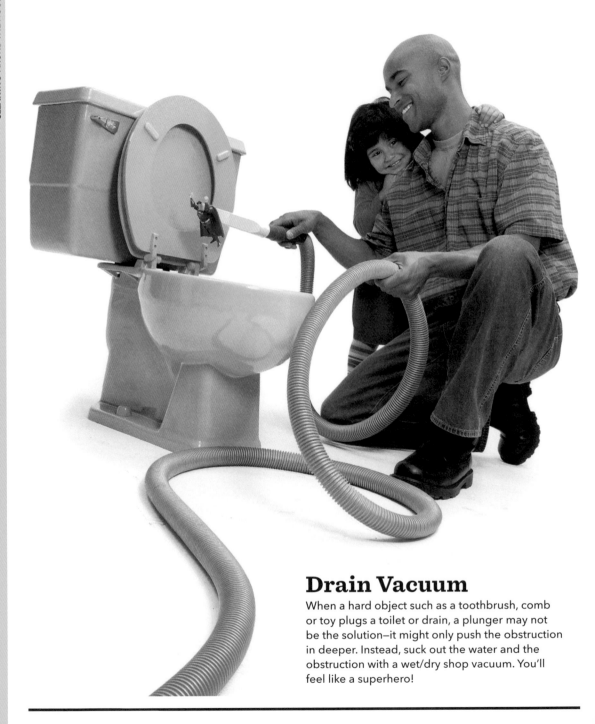

Drain Vacuum

When a hard object such as a toothbrush, comb or toy plugs a toilet or drain, a plunger may not be the solution—it might only push the obstruction in deeper. Instead, suck out the water and the obstruction with a wet/dry shop vacuum. You'll feel like a superhero!

KEEP STAINLESS STEEL STAINLESS

Stainless steel appliances look great—until they get fingerprints all over them. And while no cleaner can prevent fingerprints and smudges, the way the cleaner is applied can help avoid streaks and spotting. Instead of spraying the cleaner directly onto the surface, first spray it on a microfiber cloth and then wipe it on.

SEAL DUSTY CONCRETE

Apply a clear penetrating concrete sealer (available at home centers). One coat should do it, but you can reseal every four to five years if the dust recurs. Prepare the floor by sweeping it and then washing it with a concrete cleaner/degreaser. Any oil or grease spots will resist the sealer, so concentrate on areas where water beads up. Let the floor dry before you apply the finish. Look for water-based, low-odor products and make sure the area is well-ventilated. Read and follow the label instructions for application.

Roll-Out Workbench Dropcloth

Mount a pull-out window shade on one end of your workbench and pull it out for painting projects. Home centers will cut shades to the width you need, so measure your workbench before going to the store. Just remember: It's a good idea to wipe wet paint off the shade before rolling it back up.

Tension-rolled window shade

Scrape Away Gunk

To remove stubborn patches of dried construction adhesive from concrete, you could get down on your hands and knees and pick away at it with a putty knife. An easier and faster option is to use an oscillating tool equipped with a scraper blade. It will slice off the residue in no time.

T-shirt filter cover

DRYWALL DUST SUCKER

Vacuuming drywall dust with a shop vacuum clogs the filter fast. To make the filter stay clean longer, take an old T-shirt and cut it off just below the armholes. Then wrap the lower section around the vacuum filter and secure it with two heavy-duty rubber bands. When the T-shirt filter gets clogged, just pull it off, shake it out and reuse it.

MINI VACUUM NOZZLE

Sometimes a vacuum crevice tool isn't quite small enough, so here's a quick solution: Poke a straw-size hole in the bottom of a cup, stick a straw through a few inches, caulk the inside and outside of the cup near the straw, and let it dry. Stick the cup on your vacuum nozzle and you're all set.

Magnet In a Bag

Cleaning up metal shavings around a drill press almost always results in a metal sliver or two. Using a magnet works fine, but it's no fun to get all those shavings off. Instead, put the magnet inside a plastic bag that's turned inside out. Now you can attract the shavings to the bag, seal it and pull it free, and then throw them away without touching a single shaving.

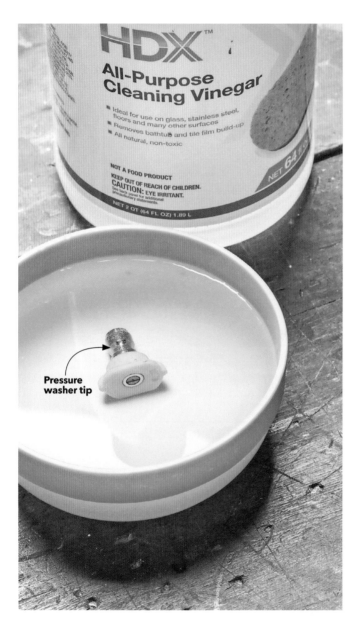

Pressure washer tip

Pressure Washer Tip Rescue

When water from a pressure washer doesn't flow properly—surging erratically or creating an odd spray pattern—it's time to clean the tip. Shove a needle into the holes to clear out what residue you can. Then soak the tip in vinegar for several hours. Pressure washers don't see as much use as a shower or kitchen faucet, but they're still susceptible to lime, scale or mineral buildup. And the tip openings are so small that a tiny obstruction can cause big problems.

LINT BUNNIES BE GONE

If you notice that it takes longer than normal for loads to dry in your clothes dryer, it may be time to clean out the vent. First detach the duct from behind the unit and then push a plumbing snake through your dryer vent from outside. Tie a rag securely to the snake end. Pull the cloth and snake through a couple of times and your clean vent will not only save energy but possibly prevent a fire as well.

REMOVE TREE SAP FROM VINYL SIDING

If drippy trees or deck lumber deposit sap on your vinyl siding, don't delay cleanup. The longer you wait, the more stubborn the sap will become. If you attack the fresh sap within a week or so, a kitchen cleaner such as Formula 409 or Fantastik will likely remove it. You can also use a biodegradable product such as Simple Green. If standard cleaners won't dissolve the sap, use a citrus cleaner such as Goo Gone. Check the label of the product you use to make sure it's recommended for vinyl; test it in an inconspicuous spot for discoloration. Apply the cleaner with a rag or sponge. Scrub off tough spots using a soft-bristle brush.

Scratch Soap to Keep Fingernails Clean

Whether you're digging in the garden or working on your car, scratch a bar of soap first. The soap will keep grunge from lodging under your fingernails. Unlike soil or grease, the soap will dissolve when you wash your hands.

CLEAN YOUR CHIMNEY

IF YOU USE your fireplace or wood stove regularly but can't remember the last time your chimney was cleaned, it's probably overdue. In many cases, you can clean the chimney yourself and save hundreds of dollars.

Removing chimney soot is pretty simple. But if you have heavy creosote buildup, you'll have to call in a pro. We'll show you how to inspect yours to see if it qualifies as a DIY job. If it does, just follow these steps. Otherwise, hire a certified chimney sweep.

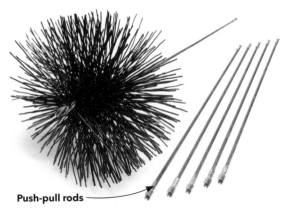

Push-pull rods

1 Buy a metal bristle brush for a clay flue liner and a brush with plastic bristles for a metal liner. Buy enough for the entire chimney height.

IS IT A DIY JOB?

Most chimney fires start in the smoke chamber or smoke shelf area, so it's the most important area to clean **(Figure A)**. Since that area is hard to reach in some fireplaces, check yours to see if you can reach into it and still have room to maneuver a brush. If you can't reach it, this isn't a DIY project.

Next, see if you can access your home's chimney crown. If you have a very steep roof pitch or aren't comfortable working on your roof, then this isn't a job for you. Call a certified chimney sweep. If you decide you can handle the heights, make sure to wear a safety harness.

DO AN INSPECTION

Strap on goggles and a respirator, clean the ashes out of the firebox, and remove the grate. Then open a door or window and wait a few minutes before opening the damper so the pressures equalize. Then open the damper and wait a few more minutes for heat to rise from the house.

Grab your brightest flashlight and a fireplace poker and lean into the firebox. Shine your light into the smoke chamber and flue and use the poker to scratch the surface. If the soot has a matte black finish and the scratch is 1/8 in. deep or less, it's a DIY job. But if the buildup is deeper or has a shiny, tarlike appearance, you have heavy creosote buildup. Stop using your fireplace immediately and call a professional chimney sweep. (See "Chimney Fires Destroy Homes.")

2 Buy a bendable "noodle brush" to clean the smoke shelf and a long-handled brush to clean soot off the sides of the firebox.

Shop vacuum hose

Canvas tarp

3 Lay a canvas tarp over the hearth and spread it into the room. Then tape poly sheeting over the fireplace and insert a shop vacuum hose. Seal everything with duct tape.

GET THE RIGHT CLEANING TOOLS

There's no "one-size-fits-all" brush for cleaning the flue. So you'll have to climb up on your roof and measure the size of your flue liner. You'll also need special brushes for the firebox and smoke

Chimney Fires Destroy Homes

Creosote buildup may not look dangerous, but it ignites at a mere 451° F, and once it starts burning, it expands like foam sealant. In less than a minute, it builds to more than 2,000° F and can engulf your entire chimney and destroy your home.

Even if you clean your chimney regularly, you should still have it inspected by a qualified chimney sweep once a year. Certified chimney sweeps are trained to recognize chimney deterioration and venting problems and can assess your chimney's condition.

Fireplace

Close door

Extra hoses taped together

Vacuum running outside

chamber areas **(Photo 2)**. Find the equipment at a home center or an online retailer such as *efireplacestore.com*.

MINIMIZE THE MESS

Before you start brushing, protect your home's interior from soot with poly sheeting, a canvas tarp and a shop vacuum **(Photo 3)**. Most shop vacuum filters can't trap all the fine soot from a fireplace, and some of it will blow right out the exhaust port. So buy extra lengths of vacuum hose and move the vacuum outside **(Photo 4)**. Then close the doors and windows on that side of your house to prevent the soot from reentering your home.

THE CLEANING PROCESS

Start the vacuum and begin cleaning at the top of the chimney **(Photo 5)**. Continue adding rods and moving down the chimney until you can't feel any more brush resistance. That means you've reached the smoke chamber and it's time to climb down from the roof and work from inside the firebox.

Peel back a small portion of the poly sheeting and use the long-handled brush to clean the smoke chamber. Use the noodle brush to remove all the soot from the smoke shelf. Then switch back to the long-handled brush to clean the sides of the firebox. Finish by vacuuming the entire firebox. Then fold up the poly sheeting and the canvas tarp and move them outside. Shake them out and reuse them the next time you clean the chimney.

4 Add sections to lengthen the vacuum hose, then connect it to your shop vacuum outside. Run the vacuum while you brush, and replace the filter when it clogs.

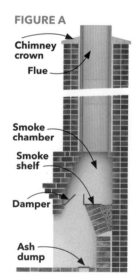

FIGURE A

Chimney crown

Flue

Smoke chamber

Smoke shelf

Damper

Ash dump

5 Ram the cleaning brush up and down several times in a small section of the flue. Use a bright flashlight to check your work before moving on to the next section.

TOP 7 PRO TIPS FOR CLEANING WINDOWS

1. USE TWO SCRUBBERS
Use one for inside and one for outside so pollutants and bird excrement stay outside.

2. CHANGE BLADES
A 12-to-14-in. squeegee is a good size for most situations. Put in a new rubber blade after each cleaning to prevent streaks.

3. USE DISH SOAP
Any kitchen dish liquid cleans dirt and grease, and leaves the glass slippery so that the squeegee glides well. Pure biodegradable soap protects sensitive plants outside, and toddlers and pets who put their mouth on the windows inside.

4. TRY A LITTLE MAGIC
Mr. Clean Magic Eraser removes silicone caulk and water drips.

5. DON'T SCRATCH IT
A razor blade removes paint overspray and gunk. Keep the glass wet and use a new blade each time. Microscopic rust particles on the blade can scratch the glass.

6. EASILY PRY OUT SCREENS
A paint can opener is perfect for popping out window screens.

7. USE TWO RAGS
Have two detailing rags on hand—one for dirty jobs such as sills and the other for detailing the edges of the glass.

CHAPTER 2

ORGANIZATION

Protect Table Leaves

When you're storing table leaves, protect the edges with pipe insulation (sold at home centers and hardware stores). It will keep your dinner table picture-perfect and free of scuffs.

WIRE CHASE

It's convenient to hang a flat screen TV on the wall and place game components below on a low table. The only downside is the bunch of unsightly cords coming down the wall. To hide the cords, build a case from plywood and paint it to match the walls. You can use 1/2-in. plywood for the back and sides, and hardboard for the front panel.

SHOE POCKET

Hanging shoe bags are great for closets, but they can also help you manage the clutter in your garage, workshop or laundry room. A shoe bag can be purchased inexpensively at discount stores.

High and Dry

When you keep your wet boots in a boot tray by the door, the boots can sit in water all day and never really get dry. Instead, elevate them from the tray using some old cooling racks. The boots will be dry when you put them on, and the water will evaporate from the tray more quickly.

Mark the Knife

Many multitools have a knife, saw, file and more, and they all look alike when the tool is folded. But for most people, 99% of the time it's the knife you want. So mark it with nail polish or paint so you can find it in an instant.

Nail polish

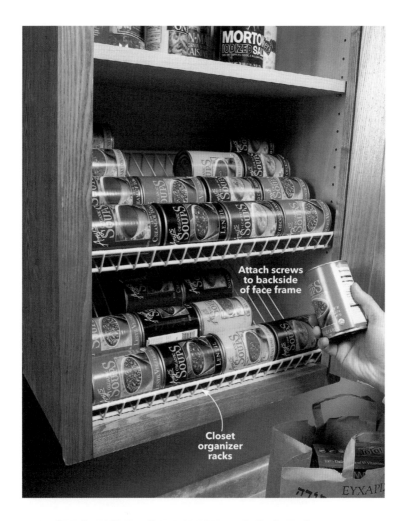

Attach screws to backside of face frame

Closet organizer racks

RACKS FOR CANNED GOODS

Use those leftover closet racks as cabinet organizers. Trim the racks to length with a hacksaw and then mount screws to the backside of the face frame to hold the racks in place. The backside of the rack simply rests against the back of the cabinet. Now you can easily find your soup and check the rest of your inventory at a glance.

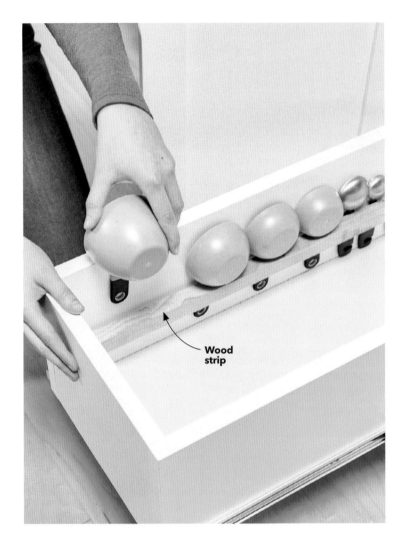

Wood
strip

DRAWER ORGANIZER

Keep measuring cups and spoons from cluttering up a drawer.
Just attach a strip of wood to the drawer's side. Install washers
behind the wood strip to create a gap for the handles to slide into.

Clever Cord Control

If you store a toaster, rice cooker or other small appliance in a cabinet, dealing with all the cords can be annoying. Here's an easy solution: Buy Command Clear Medium Cord Clips (available at home centers and amazon.com) and attach one to each appliance. Wrap the cord around the appliance and through the clip, effectively containing it. The clips are inexpensive and you can remove them without harming an appliance's paint or finish.

Drawer in a Drawer

Deep drawers often contain a jumbled pile of interlocking utensils. To organize them, add a sliding tray that creates two shallower spaces. Make it 1/8 in. narrower than the drawer box, about half the length and any depth you want (this one is 1-3/4 in. deep). When you position the holes for the adjustable shelf supports, don't rely on measurements and arithmetic. Instead, position the tray inside the drawer box at least 1/8 in. lower than the cabinet opening and make a mark on the tray. If the shelf supports don't fit tightly into the holes, use a little super glue.

Shelf
support

1/2"-thick
solid wood

1/4"
plywood

1-1/2" trim
screw

Shelf
support

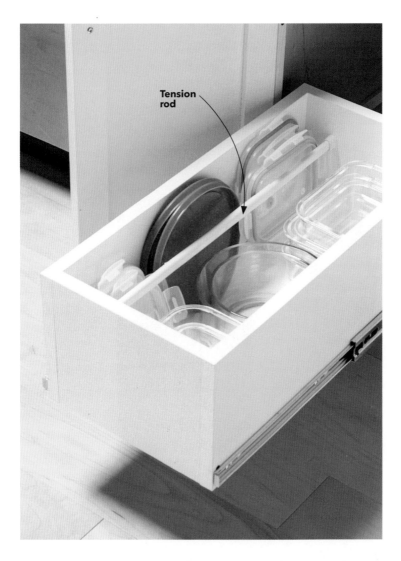

Tension rod

CORRAL THOSE CONTAINER LIDS

To keep storage container lids organized, pop a tension rod into a drawer and stand the lids up along the side.

KITCHEN WINDOW PLANT PERCH

Do you like having fresh herbs at your fingertips? Keeping them on your counter takes up valuable space and doesn't keep them exposed to enough light. Instead, install a wire shelf between the upper cabinets flanking your kitchen window. You can set your plants where they'll get plenty of light without blocking the view. This also makes watering easy and keeps them readily available for snipping. Make sure to install the shelf high enough that you don't bump into it when you're working at the sink.

Add a Shelf

Most cabinets come with only one or two shelves, leaving a lot of wasted space. You can easily gain more storage by adding one or two shelves to your cabinets. All it takes is 3/4-in. plywood and a bag of shelf supports. The supports come in two diameters, so take an existing one to the store to make sure you get the right size.

Laundry Organizer

Make laundry day easier with this shelf for all of your detergents, stain removers and other supplies. Build this simple organizer from 1x10 and 1x3 boards. If you have a basement laundry room, you may need to cut an access through the shelves for your dryer exhaust.

1x10 shelf

1-5/8" screw with finish washer

1x3 mounting strip screwed to wall

1x10 side

Sieve

UTILITY SINK SPONGE HOLDER

When wet sponges sit on the ledge of a utility sink, they never dry properly and can become moldy, smelly and unusable. To store them, screw a small sieve to the back of the sink to hold the sponges. It keeps them out of the way but provides air circulation, so they dry more quickly and last much longer. You can do a similar setup for a kitchen sink.

3/16"-dia. treated rod

3/16" nut

1/4" fender washer

STUDLY CLAMP STORAGE

Clamps scattered and hard to find when you need them most? Here's a way to keep them together. Hang bar clamps on 2x4 scraps screwed between open-wall studs. Add another board or two for glue bottles, dowels and biscuits. To hold C-clamps and spring clamps, drill holes in the studs and install lengths of 3/16-in. threaded rod, tensioned with 1/4-in. fender washers and nuts.

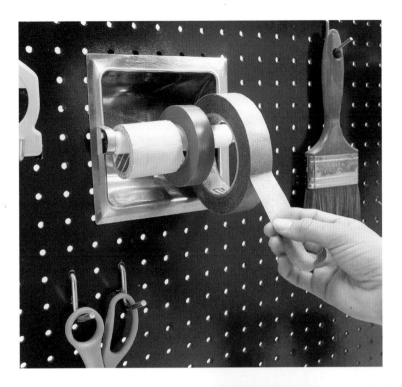

Toilet Paper Holder for Tape

An old toilet paper holder makes a handy tape dispenser for the shop. You can use a surface-mounted holder or impress the neighbors with a recessed version.

Hardware Lassos

To keep hardware neat and accessible, thread nuts, washers, sockets and other items on short pieces of 12- or 14-gauge electrical wire, and then hang them on a toolbox handle or a pegboard hook. Twist the ends of the wire into hook shapes that interlock to make it easy to close and open them.

Hijacked Tackle Box

When the fishing urge stops biting, put that old tackle box to use as a portable hardware and tool tote. Load the nifty fold-out compartments with screws, nails, bolts, tape, electrical connectors—what have you. Stash your pliers, screwdriver, wrenches, hammer, tape measure and other frequently used tools on the bottom level. When chores and repairs start nibbling at your conscience, you'll have the right tackle handy for the job.

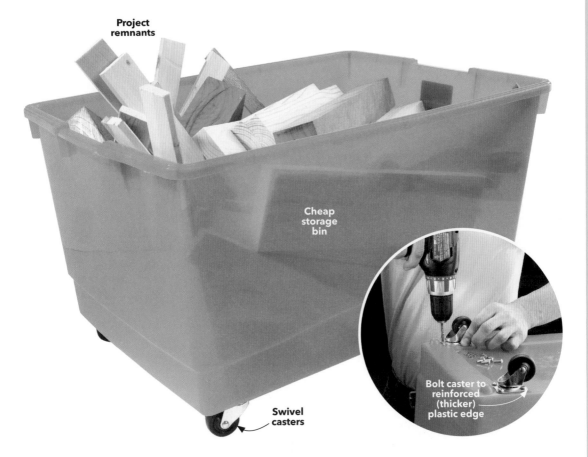

Project remnants

Cheap storage bin

Bolt caster to reinforced (thicker) plastic edge

Swivel casters

SCRAP BIN ON A ROLL

Here's a low-rolling wood scrap bin that'll capture all the cutoffs while you work on your next project. Bolt swivel casters to the base of a storage bin and it'll scoot right where you need it. Sure, you can take extra time to beef up the casters-to-bin connection by bolting plywood on before attaching the casters, but it's easier to bolt them right through the thicker, reinforced area of the bin's bottom.

JIFFY JUNK SORTING

It'll only take a second to nab the perfect-size nuts or washers from that big can loaded with 20 years' worth of leftover hardware. Pour the cargo onto a rubber car mat, rake through the pile until you find the right whatever, then use the mat as a chute to pour the heap back into the can.

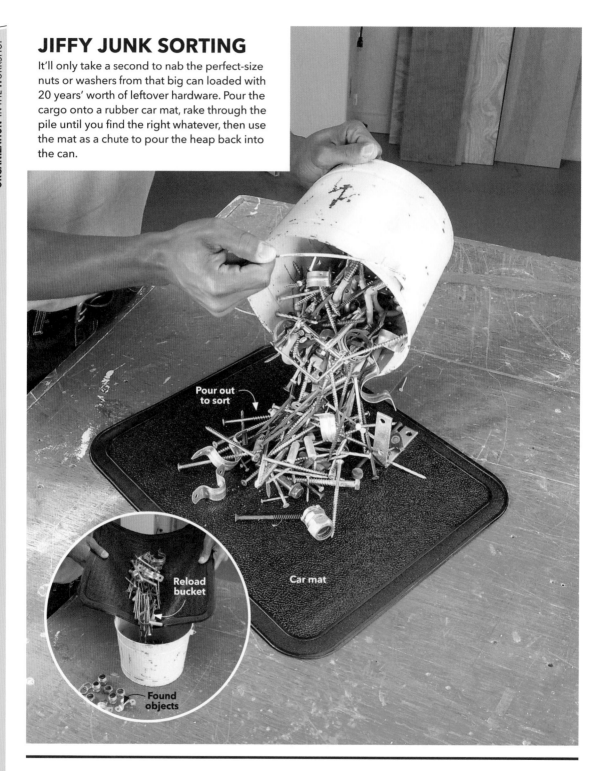

Pour out to sort

Car mat

Reload bucket

Found objects

Trim with
utility knife

64-oz. jar

Attach lid
with two
screws

28-oz. jar

Recycled Peanut Butter Jars

Plastic peanut butter jars work better for storage than glass baby food jars because they hold a lot more hardware and won't smash into slivers if you drop one. Attach the lids of 28-oz. jars under a shelf with two screws (so the lid can't spin when you loosen the jar) and screw on the loaded jar. For quick access, cut away half of a 64-oz. peanut butter jar with a sharp utility knife, leaving the neck intact, then attach the lid and jar to the side of a cabinet.

Caulk Tube Organizer

Tired of having your caulk tubes lying all over the workbench or your shelves? Make this organizer from a scrap of 2x8 and a piece of 1/4-in. plywood. Just lay out a pattern for your 2-in. hole saw to follow and drill holes through the 2x8. Then glue the plywood to the bottom. Now you can set it on a shelf and easily identify the tube you need.

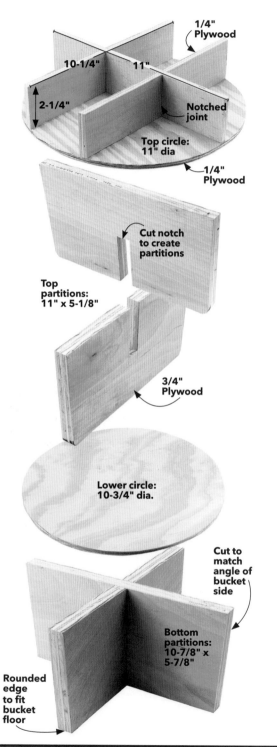

1/4"
Plywood

10-1/4"   11"

2-1/4"

Notched
joint

Top circle:
11" dia

1/4"
Plywood

Cut notch
to create
partitions

Top
partitions:
11" x 5-1/8"

3/4"
Plywood

Lower circle:
10-3/4" dia.

Cut to
match
angle of
bucket
side

Bottom
partitions:
10-7/8" x
5-7/8"

Rounded
edge
to fit
bucket
floor

Hardware Honeycomb

To organize fasteners, round up a plastic 5-gallon bucket. Use 3/4-in. plywood for the partitions and 1/4-in. plywood for the floors to match the bucket cutout dimensions shown. Cut the bucket holes with a saber saw, then saw the crisscrossing bottom partitions with slightly angled ends to fit snugly against the bucket sides. Saw notches halfway down the center of the partitions so they interlock. Next, cut the round floor to fit the bucket on top of the partition, then drop it in. Cut the next set of partitions, drop those in and then add the next floor. Create the egg carton partition to fit on top and screw or nail it to the upper floor. Then load your bucket.

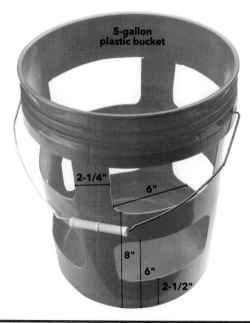

5-gallon
plastic bucket

2-1/4"   6"

8"

6"

2-1/2"

PIPE CLAMP CRADLE

This handy under-mount rack keeps your clamps right where you need them. Simply cut a series of 1-1/4-in.-diameter holes along the center line of a 2x6 and then rip the 2x6 in half to create the half-circle slots. Next, screw 1x4 sides and a top to the cradle and screw it to the bottom side of the workbench top.

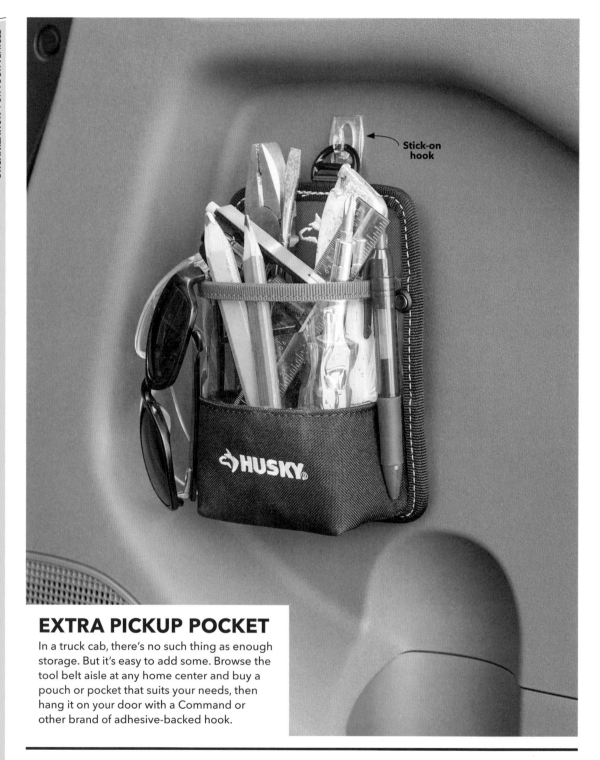

Stick-on hook

EXTRA PICKUP POCKET

In a truck cab, there's no such thing as enough storage. But it's easy to add some. Browse the tool belt aisle at any home center and buy a pouch or pocket that suits your needs, then hang it on your door with a Command or other brand of adhesive-backed hook.

GARAGE STORAGE LIFT

Build a high shelf that automatically lowers with the push of a button.

LOTS OF GARAGES are crammed full of stuff—every inch of storage space within arm's reach is used. But chances are these garages have plenty of empty space near the ceiling, and high shelving is a great option for taking advantage of that space. This shelf is convenient to access—to avoid lugging heavy bins up a ladder. For lifting power, it uses a linear actuator. The shelf glides down for easy loading, and pushing a button again lifts the shelf to the previously unused space above.

OUT-OF-THE-WAY STORAGE This shelf easily lifts and stores 450 lbs. of stuff, leaving space below for more storage or parking.

PRO TIP
Assemble this project with glue, brad nails and pocket hole screws to maximize its strength. If you don't have a pocket hole jig, use a combination of glue and screws; this shelf needs to be strong.

1 Cut and label all the parts and then assemble the shelf (**Figure A**). The cabinet (**Figure C**) doesn't get completely assembled yet; the bulkhead (**M**) is added in **Photo 9**. The back (**A**) is the last part to be attached, in **Photo 10**.

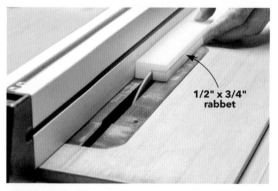

1/2" x 3/4" rabbet

2 Make L-shaped guide strips from a low-friction material called UHMW (ultra high molecular weight) plastic. They allow the shelf to slide easily as it travels up and down, and they also prevent racking from an unbalanced load. To start, make a rabbet cut on a table saw and then predrill the screw holes.

What are Linear Actuators?

A linear actuator is a small but powerful motor that moves a rod in and out. They come in various sizes and cost anywhere from less than $100 to thousands of dollars. This model has 40 in. of travel, or "stroke." It's rated to lift 450 lbs. and costs a few hundred dollars.

EASY TO INSTALL
Linear actuators are low-tech devices. If you can wire a light switch, you can wire an actuator. Most run on 12 volts, so you don't have to worry about shocking yourself. In addition to the actuator, you'll need a wireless control module and a 20-amp power supply, which adds a few hundred dollars to the cost.

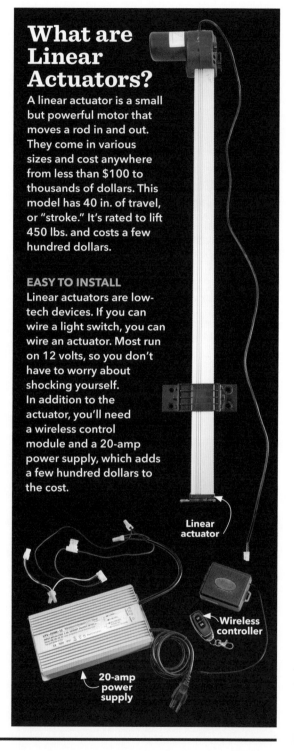

Linear actuator

Wireless controller

20-amp power supply

Cabinet

Shelf back

1-1/4"
screw

Guide
strip

3 To get the guides positioned just right, place the shelf face down on the floor and center the cabinet on top of it. Slipping the guide strips under each side of the cabinet puts them exactly where they need to be; just make sure everything is square before screwing them down.

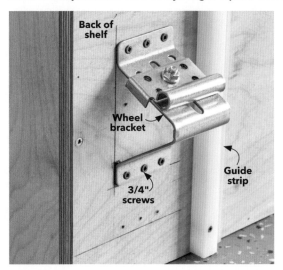

Back of
shelf

Wheel
bracket

Guide
strip

3/4"
screws

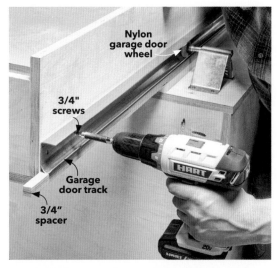

Nylon
garage door
wheel

3/4"
screws

Garage
door track

3/4"
spacer

4 On the back of the shelf, mark a line 2 in. from the edge. Mark a line 2 in. from the top and 4 in. from the bottom. With the wheels inserted, align the bracket corners with the lines; attach the brackets to the shelf with 3/4-in. screws. (Don't put the wheel brackets the same distance from the bottom and top; the lower wheels will come out of the track in the lowest position.)

5 With the curved side of the wheel track facing the front of the cabinet, slide the track over the wheels. To make sure it runs parallel to the front of the cabinet, use a strip of 3/4-in. plywood as a spacer. Then put one 3/4-in. screw near the top, one in the middle and one near the bottom of the track. More will go in, but only after it's hung on the wall.

FIGURE A
ELECTRIC SHELF

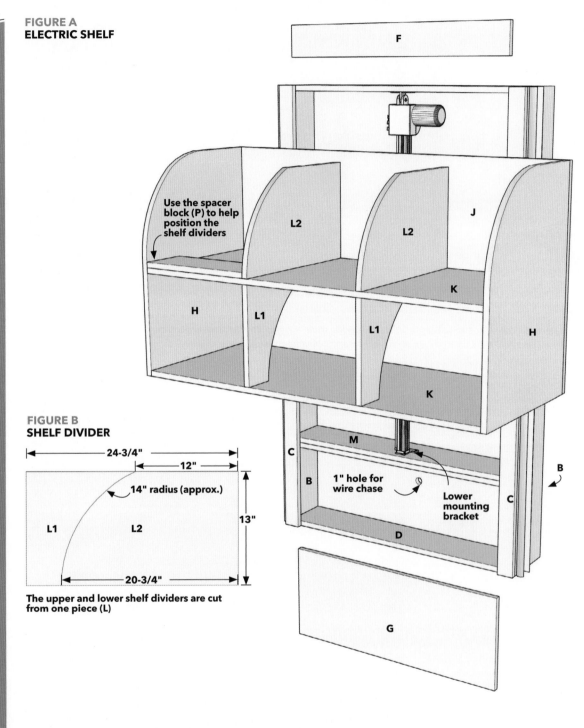

F

Use the spacer block (P) to help position the shelf dividers

L2

L2

J

H

L1

K

L1

H

K

M

C

B

B

1" hole for wire chase

Lower mounting bracket

C

B

C

D

G

FIGURE B
SHELF DIVIDER

24-3/4"

12"

14" radius (approx.)

L1

L2

13"

20-3/4"

The upper and lower shelf dividers are cut from one piece (L)

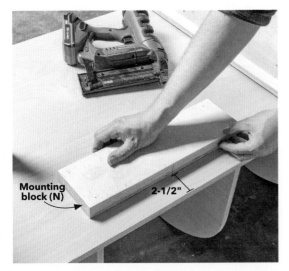

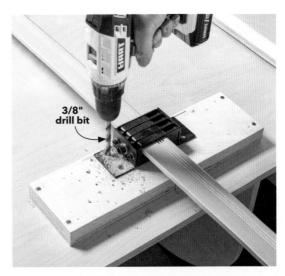

6 To strengthen the shelf, center one mounting block **(N)** exactly 2-1/2 in. from the top of the shelf and attach it with wood glue and 1-1/4-in. screws. Use the same method to stack the second mounting block on top of the first.

7 With the shelf and cabinet still face down and the actuator positioned with the carriage centered on the mounting blocks **(N)**, use the brackets of the carriage itself as a guide to drill 3/8-in. holes through the mounting blocks into the shelf.

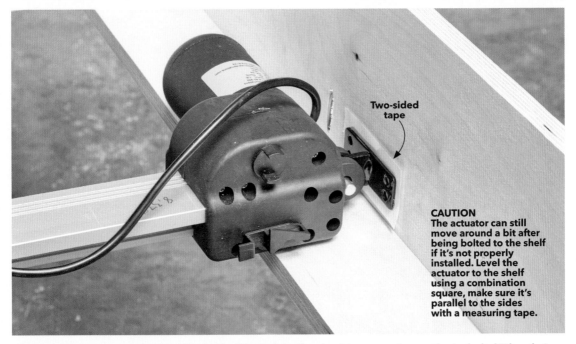

CAUTION
The actuator can still move around a bit after being bolted to the shelf if it's not properly installed. Level the actuator to the shelf using a combination square, make sure it's parallel to the sides with a measuring tape.

8 With the actuator bolted to the shelf, slide the shelf and cabinet together so the included T-bracket would touch the cabinet top. The tape on the T-bracket keeps it perfectly positioned while you remove the clevis pin and get the actuator out of the way. Use 3/4-in. screws to complete the job.

FIGURE C
SHELF CABINET

SHOPPING FOR MATERIALS
Most of the materials for this project are available at home centers, but some things are easier to find online. The garage door tracks and wheels can be ordered from *americandoorsupply.com* and the linear actuator kit from *progressiveautomations.com*. Look for the UHMW plastic at a local Woodcraft store.

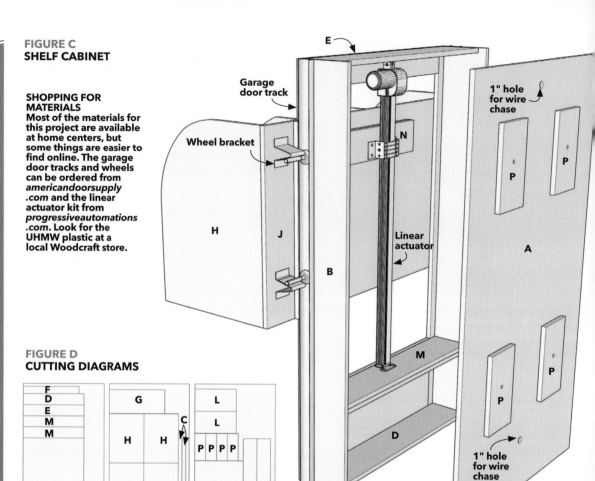

FIGURE D
CUTTING DIAGRAMS

CUTTING LIST

KEY	QTY.	SIZE & DESCRIPTION
A	1	3/4" x 64" x 36" (Cabinet back)
B	2	3/4" x 64" x 8" (Cabinet sides)
C	2	3/4" x 64" x 2-1/4" (Cabinet stiles)
D	1	3/4" x 36" x 6-1/2" (Cabinet bottom)
E	1	3/4" x 36" x 6-1/2" (Cabinet top)
F	1	3/4" x 33" x 4-1/4" (Cabinet rail top)
G	1	3/4" x 33" x 14" (Access panel)
H	2	3/4" x 29" x 20-3/4" (Shelf sides)
J	1	3/4" x 51" x 29" (Shelf back)
K	2	3/4" x 49-1/2" x 20-3/4" (Shelf bottom)
L	2	3/4" x 24-3/4" x 13" (Divider blanks)
M	2	3/4" x 36" x 6-1/2" (Bulkhead)
N	2	3/4" x 17-1/2" x 5" (Mounting blocks)
P	4	3/4" x 16" x 6-1/2" (Spacer blocks)

MATERIALS LIST

ITEM	QTY.
40" linear track actuator	1
12V power supply and controller	1
Actuator control module	1
4' x 8' sheets of plywood	3
3/4" x 36" UHMW plastic	1
6' garage door tracks	2
Garage door wheels with bearings	4
3/4" wood screws	1 box
1-1/4" wood screws	1 box
1-1/4" brass trim-head screws	4 ea.
3/8-16 x 3" lag bolts and locknuts	4 ea.

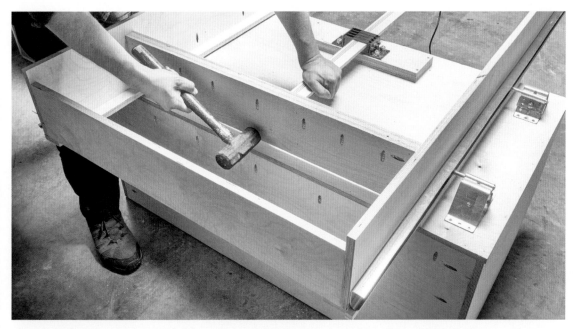

9 Once the T-bracket is screwed on, reattach the actuator, put the bulkhead (**M**) in place and hit it with a hammer. This presses the screw heads of the lower mounting bracket into the plywood so the bulkhead can sit flush with it.

Spacer block (P)

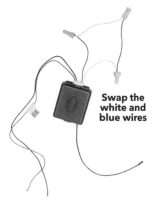

Swap the white and blue wires

11 Since the actuator is mounted upside-down, you need to swap the lead wires so that the carriage runs the correct way when the up or down button is pushed on the remote. All you need to do is cut and swap the white and blue wires coming from the control box.

10 Use the same spacer blocks (**P**) that space the dividers in the shelf. This time use them along the inside of the cabinet to keep the back from sagging while you screw it in.

MAKE SURE IT'S SECURE
This shelf is heavy! To make sure you anchor into studs, predrill two holes in the cabinet back near the top and two near the bottom, horizontally spaced 24 in. on center. As the final task for the spacer blocks (P), fasten them over the holes on the back of the cabinet using glue and 1-1/4-in. screws.

Temporary stand made from 2x4s

12 Make a support stand from scrap wood and position the cabinet against the wall. Drive in one lag screw. Have one person check for plumb and the other drive in the remaining three lag bolts. After securing the cabinet to the wall, remove the middle and lower screws from the wheel rails.

13 The shelf can't slide straight up into position; the mounting blocks on the back of the shelf won't clear the bottom of the cabinet. With a helper on the other side, swing the rails out just enough to guide the wheels into them. Once the shelf is lifted high enough, swing it back in, and while your helper keeps it steady, line up the bolt holes to the actuator carriage.

Snug the wheel to the track and tighten the bolt

14 With the shelf installed, plug in the electronics and test the movement of the shelf. (Look at the guide strips as it moves; if you notice a gap, adjust the upper wheels a little tighter to the shelf.)

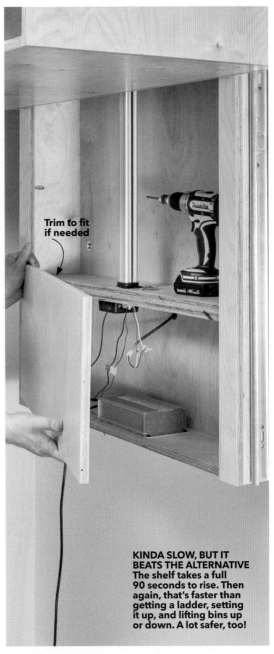

Trim to fit if needed

KINDA SLOW, BUT IT BEATS THE ALTERNATIVE
The shelf takes a full 90 seconds to rise. Then again, that's faster than getting a ladder, setting it up, and lifting bins up or down. A lot safer, too!

15 Install the power supply and the receiver in the lower section of the cabinet. Use brass trim-head screws to attach the access panel **(G)**. (You might need to cut the panel down to fit.)

WORKSHOP STORAGE

Quick and simple ways to get organized

Vinyl Gutter Tool Tray

What can you do with a leftover length of gutter? You can screw it to the edge of your workbench and use it to keep tools and fasteners out of your way but handy for assembly work.

Cordless Drill Hangout

Screw large vinyl-covered hooks (sold at hardware stores and home centers) to a convenient spot on a wall or exposed stud and hang up those drills for safekeeping and easy access.

Round Up Small Parts

Steel shower curtain holders are perfect for organizing small hardware with holes, such as saber saw blades, washers, eye screws, POP rivet parts and cotter pins.

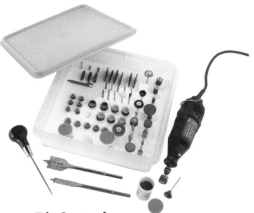

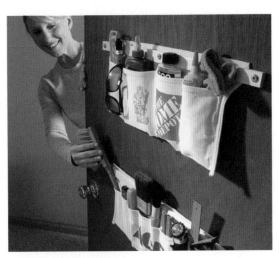

Rotary Bit Organizer

If you avoid using your rotary tool because all the bits and accessories are a discouraging mess, here is a solution for you: Friction-fit a piece of 3/4-in. plastic foam into a snap-lid plastic food container. Then poke holes in the foam with an awl to hold shafted bits, and slice crevices with a utility knife to hold cutoff discs. Using a spade bit at high speed, drill sockets for larger bits and tube-shape containers. Then just load it up and snap it shut.

Tool-Apron Storage

Tool aprons can be modified to store nearly any household item. Just sew a variety of pocket widths in the apron, then mount them by screwing a wood strip through the top of each and into a door. For hollow-core doors, use drywall fasteners to hold the screws firmly to the door.

CHAPTER 3

MAINTENANCE

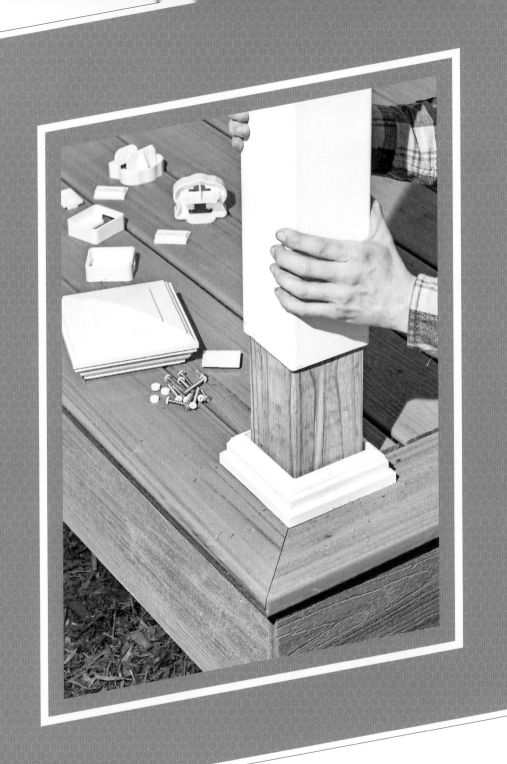

CIRCUIT BREAKER ID

When you need to turn off the power to a circuit, there's no need to flip circuit breakers on and off until you find the right one. To end the guesswork, just write the corresponding circuit breaker number on the backs of the outlet covers and switch plates.

Renew Your Vinyl Floors

Vinyl plank flooring is durable, easy to install and beautiful. However, it's not immune to scratches, and a little dirt underfoot can mar that beauty. You can make scratches disappear by rubbing with sandpaper. Use a little water to lubricate the sandpaper. Start at 120 grit, then move to 180, and stop at 220. Be sure to test first in an inconspicuous spot to make sure the vinyl reacts well to sanding.

Scratch

Make Leftover Paint Last

Sooner or later, all paints go bad in storage. And this is especially true if only a quart is left in the bottom of a gallon can. But it can be avoided. Leftover paint should be poured into a mason jar and labeled. This will greatly reduce the paint's exposure to oxygen and keep it fresh and ready to use when touch-ups are needed.

DIY COVERED LITTER BOX

Make your own covered litter box and save some money. Mark an opening on one end of a large plastic storage container, then push a sharp razor knife into the plastic and cut out the opening. Pour in the litter and your cat will figure out the rest.

STEAM-IRON CLEAN-OUT

Got a steam iron that won't steam? Chances are it's clogged with mineral deposits. Fill the iron with white vinegar instead of water. Then set it flat on an oven rack and let it steam away. By the time the vinegar is steamed out, your iron should be clean.

Stop Drawer Fallout

Self-closing cabinet door hinges screwed to drawer backs can act as stops to prevent drawers from being pulled all the way out and dumping their contents on the floor. Just screw the hinges to the backs of the drawer boxes. Flip the hinge leaves down so you can slide the drawer into place and then flip them up. Purchase a pair of inexpensive self-closing hinges at home centers or hardware stores.

Rubber band

Light shade

No-Rattle Ceiling Fan

If the screws that hold the light globe to your ceiling fan tend to work loose and then hum or rattle, slip a wide rubber band around the neck of the globe where the screws grip it. The rubber band prevents the screws from loosening, dampens any noise and protects the globe from overzealous screw tighteners.

STOP LOSING SOCKS

Narrow spaces around laundry room appliances are a magnet for socks. Block them off by stuffing a strip of foam pipe insulation into the openings. That way, socks can't slip into the abyss.

WOOD FLOOR SAVER

Prevent your rocking chair from damaging your wood floor by running two strips of cloth adhesive tape along the bottom of each rocker. Not only does it help protect the floor but it also keeps the chair from sliding around and makes it quieter.

Twist the Fins to Silence a Whistling Grille

If you have a grille or register that hums or howls, all you have to do to silence it is twist the fins and open them a little. A pliers alone will scratch and kink the delicate fins, so apply electrical tape to a hinge that's about the same length as the fins. Then grab each fin between the hinge leaves and twist slightly.

Clog Claw

Before you remove the drain trap to get at that stubborn clog, try to yank out the clog with a flexible-shaft pick-up tool. You can buy one at a home center.

Tightening Plastic Nuts

A toilet supply line with a metal nut or reinforced plastic compression nut is a better choice than one with a regular plastic nut. But if you can't find one, you can tighten a plastic nut this way: First, tighten it just enough to stop leaks. Come back a few hours later when the rubber gasket has compressed a bit and snug it up a tad more. Don't crank on it with pliers. You could strip the threads or crack the nut.

MAINTAIN YOUR GARBAGE DISPOSAL

In-sink disposals get fed a lot of things (including some things they shouldn't). To keep yours lubricated and running smoothly, pour in a squirt of dish soap and run it. Once a month, grind up ice cubes to help keep the blades free of rust.

NEW ANGLES ON TOOL SHARPENING

Hold tools securely while grinding them and create the right bevel angle by using a short piece of 2x4 with an angled end and a 1-1/4-in. hole for a clamp. Make one for chisels and plane blades, and others with different angles for wood-turning tools. Label them so you know which blocks are for which tools. For a Delta grinder with a 6-in.-diameter wheel, a 5-1/2-in.-long piece of 2x4 aligns the tool to the wheel just right. For other grinders, you may need to adjust this length. To determine the block angle (it's not the same as the tool's bevel angle), turn off the grinder and hold the tool's bevel flush against the wheel. The angle of the tool shaft to the workbench is the angle to cut on the 2x4.

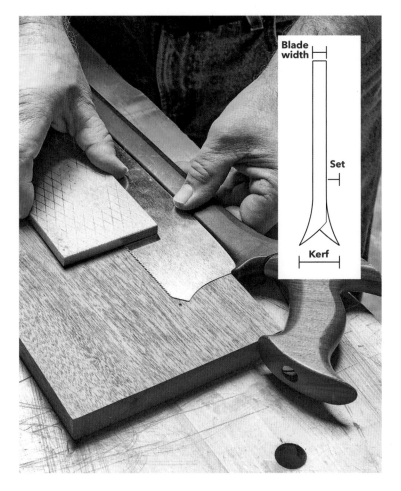

Blade
width

Set

Kerf

Align Your Saw Teeth

When a saw doesn't want to cut a straight line, the teeth might be
to blame. Most saw teeth have a "set," which is how far the teeth stick
out on either side of the blade. When the teeth stick out farther on
one side than on the other, the blade will drift in that direction. To
correct the problem, very lightly grind down the protruding teeth
with a sharpening stone. One stroke will often be enough.

UNCLOG A NOZZLE

When a spray nozzle is clogged—or partially clogged, so that the paint just sputters out—soak it in a jar of acetone or nail polish remover. Use a glass jar, since these strong solvents will destroy some types of plastic. Cap the jar and let the solvent work for a few hours.

SLICK TABLE SAW

The best way to protect a cast-iron table saw top is to occasionally rub on a coat of paste wax. This gives a nice, slick top for easier material feeding, and if you drip glue on the surface, it won't stick. It also helps prevent surface rust when the air is humid.

Flag Your Lawn Problems

When you cut grass with a riding mower, you may run across problems such as weeds or ant hills that you can't deal with right away. To remember them, keep a supply of marking flags—sometimes called stake or irrigation flags—on hand (they're inexpensive and sold at home centers). Then just stick one in the ground wherever you encounter a problem. After you're done mowing, you can easily find the spots in your lawn that need attention.

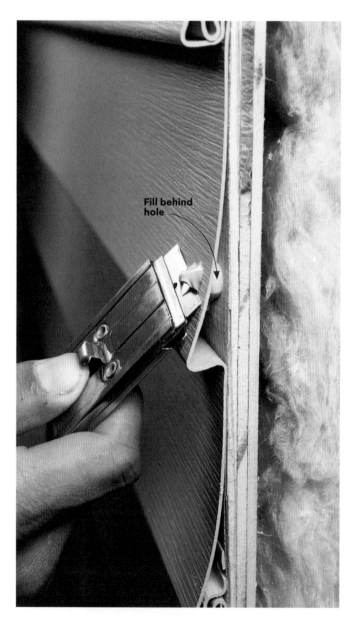

Fill behind hole

Color-matched caulk

REPAIR HOLES IN ALUMINUM AND VINYL SIDING

For an easy fix that keeps water out and is almost invisible from several feet away, fill the hole with a color-matched caulk. Siding wholesalers that sell to contractors carry caulks specifically blended for dozens of different shades of siding. Before filling the hole, wipe the siding clean. Squirt enough caulk into the hole to fill the area behind it. Avoid smearing excess caulk all over the surrounding siding—the less you get on the siding, the less obvious the repair will be. Once the caulk is fully cured (which could be several days, depending on the type), trim it even with the siding with a razor blade.

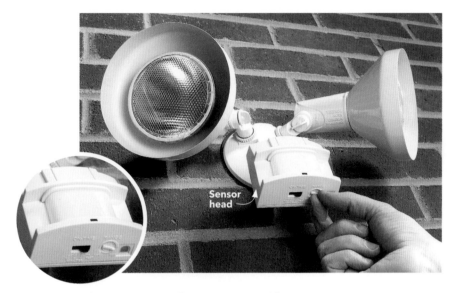

Sensor head

Tame a Hyperactive Motion Detector

If passing cars or the neighbor's pets trigger a motion detector light, adjust the detection zone–the area where the sensor can see moving objects. First, aim the detector. Turn the sensor head right or left and up or down so that its field of vision is roughly centered on the area you want to cover; tighten the screws or ring nuts on the sensor head arm. Next, set the "on-time" switch to "test." Determine the detection zone by walking across the detector's field of vision. When it sees you, the light will go on for a couple of seconds. (Your detector may need a brief warm-up period before it works.) If the detection zone is too long, aim the head down slightly. If it's too short, raise the head but keep it at least 1 in. from lightbulbs and lamp covers. When the range is about right, make finer adjustments using the range (or sensitivity) dial. Set it at the maximum range and turn it down to shorten the zone. If the zone is still too wide, narrow the lens opening with electrical tape. This is a trial-and-error process that can take a few minutes. Normally, you need to apply tape only to the right or left ends of the lens, but you can cover as much of the lens as you like. When the length and width of the zone are right, reset the on-time switch.

Use auger tip screws, because they don't require predrilling

Replace a Worn-Out Side Table

The side table on grills can rust over time. Rather than replacing it with a new metal table, use a bamboo cutting board instead. Use the old side table as a template and trace its shape on the bamboo. Make a quick cut on a band saw and screw it on. It looks fantastic! To keep it that way, apply butcher block oil at the beginning of every grilling season.

REBUILD A CONCRETE CORNER

To repair a crumbled corner, assemble an L-shaped wooden form, lock it into place with bricks and fill the void with concrete repair mix. A repair mix will stick to the old concrete better than standard concrete mix. If you don't want to buy a special edging tool to round the edges of the patch, carefully shape the edges with a putty knife.

Edging tool

Form

ALWAYS USE NEW GAS

Small engines love fresh fuel. If you have a can of gas that's been sitting around for more than four months, recycle that old fuel. Ethanol blends have an even shorter life. Through oxidation and evaporation, gasoline becomes less combustible, leading to poor performance, rough idling and varnish deposits.

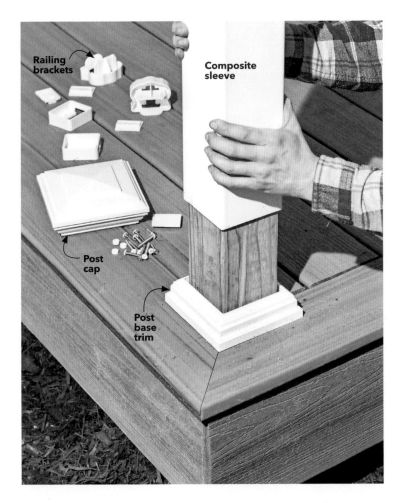

Railing brackets

Composite sleeve

Post cap

Post base trim

Update Wood Posts with a Sleeve

To protect your wood posts and give them a new look fast, you can just slide a sleeve over the top. Combine them with an 8-ft. railing kit and you'll get a maintenance-free, relatively inexpensive section of railing and posts. Find the sleeves and railing kits at home centers.

REPLACE A BROKEN TILE

If you have leftover tile or can find new tile to match your old, your floor can look as good as new in a couple of days.

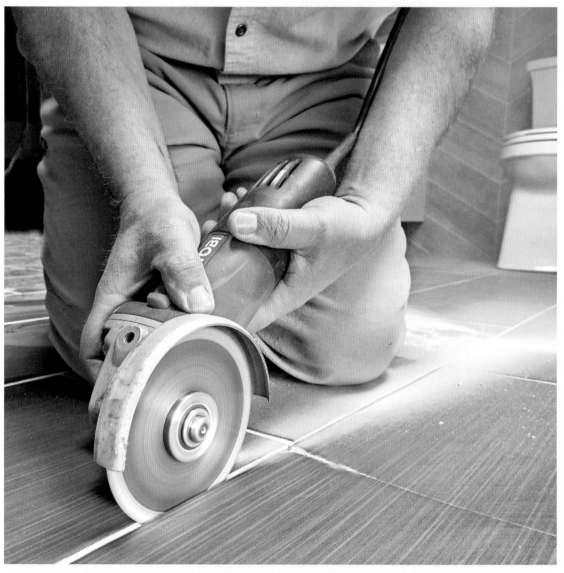

1 Using an angle grinder with a masonry wheel, cut through the grout down to the subfloor all around the tile. Using a chisel and hammer could crack adjoining grout lines.

2 Poke a screwdriver tip into the crack and pry up the damaged tile. Don't pry against a good tile; you risk damaging it, too. Chip out any remaining tile and mortar. A cheap wood chisel is perfect for this and for trimming out any remaining grout up to the edges of the good tile.

3 Mix up a small batch of mortar and spread it in the tile area with a notched trowel of the correct size. For large-format tile, use a 1/4-in. x 3/8-in. notch. Set the new tile in place, pressing it into the mortar so it's level with the surrounding tiles. Allow the mortar to set for 24 hours.

Grout float

4 After the mortar has set, grout the joints with a grout float. For a close match, use the grout originally used, thought it may not be quite the same color as the surrounding grout due to aging and foot traffic.

5 Wipe off any excess grout with a damp sponge, frequently rinsing it out. Wipe down the grout lines, applying enough pressure to make them level with the surrounding lines. Let the grout set for 24 hours before walking on it.

FLUSH A WATER HEATER

HAVE YOU FLUSHED your water heater lately? This boring but important chore should be done at least once a year to remove sediment that accumulates on the bottom of the tank. That's especially true if you live in a hard-water area. The task is easy to blow off because it's out of sight—but skipping it is costing you a lot. Sediment buildup reduces the heating efficiency of your water heater.

ALL ABOUT SEDIMENT
One sign of excessive sediment buildup is a popping or rumbling sound coming from your water heater. That's the sound of steam bubbles percolating up through the muck. On a gas water heater, the sediment creates hot spots that can damage the tank and cause premature failure. On an electric water heater, sediment buildup can cause the lower heating element to fail. So flushing offers a payback in lower energy bills and extended heater life.

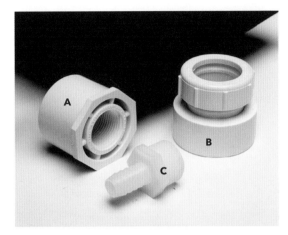

1 Glue a 1-1/2-in. PVC x 3/4-in. FIP adapter **(A)** onto a female PVC trap adapter **(B)**. This allows you to attach your vacuum to 3/4-in. pipe (see below). The barbed fitting **(C)** connects to tubing **(Photo 4)**.

TPR valve

Vacuum hose 2-1/2" to 1-1/4" reducers

Vacuum adapter in TPR port

2 Remove the temperature pressure release valve and screw in the vacuum adapter. Attach the shop vacuum hose and fire up the vacuum.

Full-port valve

Garden hose adapter

3 Unscrew the old drain valve and install the full-port valve (closed position). Attach one end of the garden hose to the valve and run the other end into a colander and on to the floor drain.

However, if you've never flushed your water heater, or haven't done it in years, you could be in for a nasty surprise. As soon as you open the drain valve, the sediment will likely clog it and prevent you from closing the valve all the way after it's drained. Then you'll have sediment buildup and a leaking water heater. We'll show you the best way to drain the sediment out of even the most neglected heater and save you a service call. You'll need some inexpensive plumbing parts, a garden hose, a wet vacuum, pliers and a pipe wrench.

BUY THE PARTS

Not only will an old drain clog up, but you won't be able to suck debris through its small opening. The key is to build a new drain valve with a 3/4-in. full-port brass ball valve with threaded ends, a 3-in. x 3/4-in. galvanized nipple, and a 3/4-in. MIP x G.H. garden hose adapter (one choice is the BrassCraft No. HU22-12-12TP).

Then build a shop vacuum adapter. If your shop vacuum has a 2-1/2-in. hose, buy a converter to reduce it to 1-1/4-in. (the Shop-Vac No. 9068500 is one option). Then assemble a vacuum-hose-to-plumbing adapter **(Photo 1)** with a 1-1/4-in. x 1-1/2-in. female PVC trap adapter, a 3/4-in. MIP x 1/2-in. barb fitting, a second 3/4-in. x 3-in. nipple and a 24-in. piece of 1/2-in. I.D. vinyl tubing.

START THE DRAINING PROCESS

Shut off the gas or electricity to the water heater, open a hot water faucet and let it run full blast for about 10 minutes to reduce the water temperature in the tank. Then shut off the cold water valve at the top of the tank and attach a garden hose to the existing drain valve and route it to a floor drain. (Use a kitchen colander to catch the sediment so it doesn't clog the floor drain.) Then open a hot water faucet on an upper floor and the water heater drain valve. Let the tank drain until sediment clogs the valve and reduces the flow. Then close the upstairs hot water faucet and water heater drain valve.

Next, remove the clogged drain valve and swap in the new full-port valve. But first, remove the blow-off tube and the temperature pressure release (TPR) valve and apply suction to the tank so that you won't get soaked when you yank the old drain valve **(Photo 2)**. Then swap the valves **(Photo 3)**. Remove the vacuum hose from the TPR port and then finish draining the tank.

Most of the sediment will flush out through the full-port valve. To remove the rest, open the cold water valve at the top of the tank in short bursts to blast it toward the drain. If you still can't get the last bit out, try vacuuming it **(Photo 4)**.

When you're done, close the ball valve and leave it in place. But remove the lever handle to prevent accidental opening. Then reinstall the TPR valve and blow-off tube. Refill the water heater and turn on the gas or electricity, and you'll be back in hot water without all the noise.

4 Remove the full-port valve and suck out the remaining sediment with your shop vacuum adapter and vinyl tubing.

WATER SOFTENER 101

YOUR WATER SOFTENER is easily the most ignored appliance in your house. You don't interact with it as you do with your range, refrigerator, or washer and dryer. It might also be the most misunderstood. You put salt in (when you remember), but do you know how it works, what it's doing and whether it's performing the way it should? Here's a quick tutorial in water softeners.

HOW DOES A WATER SOFTENER WORK?

In the simplest terms, a water softener is a filtering device for your home's water supply. It removes high concentrations of minerals, such as calcium and magnesium, which can cause buildup in your home's pipes, plumbing fixtures and water heater.

Most water softener systems use resin beads as a filtration media in a process called ion exchange. The ion-exchange beads in your water softener's resin tank are negatively charged. Hard water minerals such as calcium, magnesium and iron each have a positive charge. When those positive minerals pass through the softener, they're trapped by the negative resin, leaving you with softened water at the faucets.

When the resin beads fill up with minerals and contaminants, they no longer carry a negative charge. To recharge them, the system initiates a cleaning cycle. A saltwater solution from the main tank rinses over the beads to flush the contaminants out of the resin and down the drain. The beads return to their negative charge and are ready to soften water again.

Calcium & magnesium ions in untreated water

Sodium ions

Ion exchange resin

Calcium & magnesium ions

Sodium ions in treated water

HOW CAN I TELL IF MY SOFTENER IS WORKING EFFICIENTLY?

A telltale sign of hard water is the scaly white residue that can build up around the mouth of a faucet. This residue may also show up on shower walls, toilets and water-dependent appliances. These calcium and magnesium deposits can destroy the plumbing in a home, and that's why

Testing the Waters

Homeowners with water softeners can and should test their water using hard water test strips, available at most hardware stores. Use water that has not gone through the softener, such as water from an outdoor tap or faucet. "With more than 85% of North American households in a hard water area, homeowners who add a water softener should see a noticeable improvement shortly after installation," says Mike Bruce, Senior Product Development Manager at Rheem Manufacturing. "If your dishes and glassware are spotty or if you find soap scum on your shower walls, you will benefit from a water softener."

There's a growing focus on water softeners as a significant contributor of chloride to our rivers and lakes. Bruce says, "The industry is developing technology that can mitigate the environmental impact of water softener use. Some municipalities are shifting to up-front methods of softening (i.e., lime-softening) the water supply before it reaches residents' homes. Residents in these areas will see lower hardness levels when testing and may not need to install a softener."

Soft water

Hard water

Maintenance

BUY GOOD-QUALITY SALT
Use pure salt with an iron remover. Standard rock salt is less expensive, but it contains contaminants that can be hard on your water softener. Rock salt can cause inches of sediment to build up in the brine tank, and the sediment can clog the injector and the softener's control valve.

MAINTAIN THE SALT LEVELS
Quality salt typically improves a water softener's efficiency, but maintaining sufficient salt levels is crucial to ensure your device operates at its best.

CLEAN THE BRINE TANK ANNUALLY
Solid masses of salt, known as bridges, can result from adding too much salt or adding it too frequently. You can break up these masses with a broom handle or dissolve them with hot water. Empty the tank annually and remove any sediment with a shop vacuum. Use soap and water to thoroughly clean the tank, then rinse it.

CLEAN THE RESIN BED
Bruce recommends using a water softener cleaner once a year because it removes iron to clean the resin bed. More ambitious DIYers can clean the resin tank injector and the parts in the control valve.

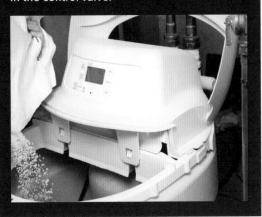

your water softener needs to function properly. One of the things new users notice when using a water softener is that their water can feel silkier and they can shower or bathe with less soap. Also, if you've been using softened water previously and your water starts to feel slimy, you should check your softener's salt levels to ensure the appliance is functioning properly. Also check that no other contaminants are affecting your home's water. You can always have your water tested by a state-certified laboratory. You can find one in your area by calling the Safe Drinking Water Hotline at (800) 426-4791 or visiting *epa.gov/safewater/labs*.

CHAPTER 4

SAFETY &
SECURITY

3-1/2"
remodeler
outlet box

Coax cable
box cover

OUTLET BOX SAFE

Fake wall outlets make terrific "safes." You can purchase them but they
are easy (and cheaper) to make yourself. Cut a hole in drywall, install a
3-1/2-in.-deep remodeler outlet box and screw on a coax cable cover
for a convenient little handle. Now you have a secret place to stash
cash and jewelry where no thieves would ever think to look.

Check Your Fire Extinguishers

Experts recommend you have an extinguisher on each level of your home and in your garage. Once in place, it's easy to forget about them, but they don't last forever. If you've had your extinguisher for a while, check the expiration date on the label. Also make sure the pressure gauge reads "full."

Control Hazardous Dust

Concrete contains crystalline silica, which can lead to very serious health issues if inhaled. Always wear a respirator when drilling concrete. But don't stop there: A vacuum nozzle close to the action prevents most of the dust from ever getting into the air.

QUICK REFERENCE GUIDE

Keep a straightforward how-to reference guide attached to any tool that requires a series of steps to operate safely. Write concise instructions on an index card. Strengthen the paper by laminating it with packing tape. Finish by punching a hole and cable-tying the guide to the device.

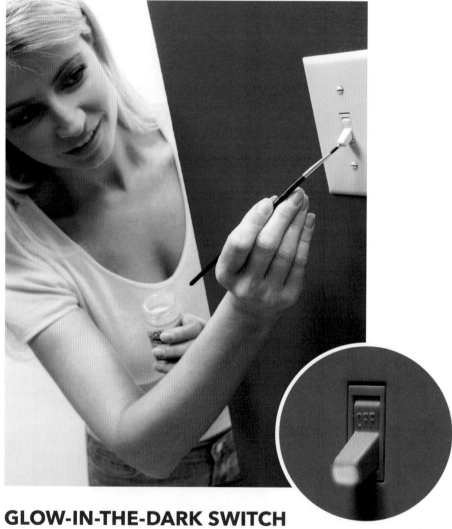

GLOW-IN-THE-DARK SWITCH

A dab of glow-in-the-dark paint applied to the tip of a light switch means no more groping for the switch at night. The paint dries clear and glows for about eight hours after exposure to light. You can find the paint at a paint or craft store.

Old Eyeglasses for Messy Jobs

Construction is hard on eyeglasses. When you get new glasses, save the old pair. Wear them instead of your new ones when you have to do messy work such as demolition or slithering around in crawl spaces. They're also good for jobs that could splatter stuff on lenses, such as painting a ceiling.

Shut Off the Water

If you're leaving town for a few days or more, turn the water off at the main shutoff. That way, if a pipe does freeze and crack, you'll have far less damage. Also shut off your automatic ice maker so that it doesn't continually try to make ice, burning out the motor. Even if the ice bin is full, the ice will evaporate and the ice maker will try to make more.

Main shutoff

Noncontact voltage tester

TEST YOUR TESTER

When you're testing an outlet or circuit you suspect is dead, first use your tester on a circuit you know is live, to verify that the tester is working. Then, after testing the suspect circuit, recheck the tester on the good circuit. This ensures that your tester is working before you check a suspect circuit, and that it's still working afterward. It only takes a few seconds and could save your life.

ADD SECURITY WITH A DOOR BLOCKER

If you don't like the look of the metal plates that protect doors from break-ins, consider adding a Prime-Line door blocker (No. U-10826, sold at home centers). TA burglar can't kick in a door equipped with this kind of lock. However, you can only operate the blocker from inside the house, so it adds security only when you're home.

Write Down the Install Date

Smoke alarms should be changed every 10 years. Most manufacturers list the date a smoke alarm was made on the back. That's helpful information if you remember to look for it. Give yourself a proper reminder and write the date you installed the alarm in big, bold numbers either on the base plate, so you'll notice it every time you change the batteries, or on the inside of the cover.

Bandsaw Blade Hangers

If you've ever suffered the indignity—and possible danger to the eyes and face—of a bandsaw blade uncoiling as you've pulled it off the peg you hung it on, you'll love this tip. Nest the coiled blades into binder clips and store them on your pegboard. They'll never spring out at you again. Apply labels to the clip so you can make it easy to select the right size and organize them.

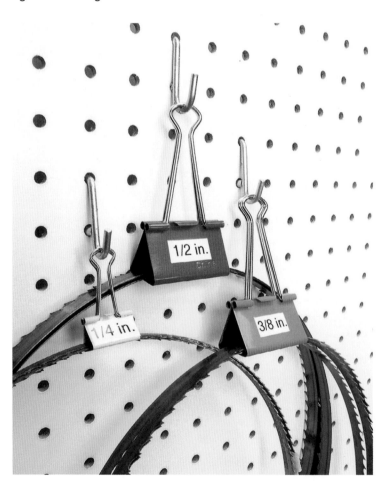

VIBRATION MITIGATION

If vibrating tools leave you with aching joints, wear a pair of cycling gloves. The gel-filled palms are designed to absorb vibration. They're sold at bike stores but you may also find them at discount stores.

FINGER-SAVING NAIL HOLDER

If you build small projects such as wren and bluebird houses, you probably use lots of small nails that can be hard to grip to start them. Try this: Trim back the lid from a small peanut can and drill a small hole near the end. Then cut a slit leading away from the hole so when you pull the lid back it releases from the nail.

Cut Small Parts Safely

Dowel screw

When cutting small furniture legs on a miter saw, their irregular shape can make it impossible to hold them safely. Instead, attach each leg to a scrap 2x2 with a dowel screw. The assembly stays straight and keeps your hands far from the blade.

Whack on Bubble Wrap

For kids who aren't quite ready to drive nails but want to use a hammer, give them some bubble wrap and a kid-size hammer or rubber mallet. (Hearing protection is a good idea. This gets LOUD.)

TABLE SAW SAFETY TIPS

The table saw is arguably the most dangerous power tool in the shop even when you're using it for crosscutting. Here are a few tips to keep you as safe as possible.

- Always unplug the saw when you're squaring up the blade with a drafting square.
- Make sure the safety guard support lines up with the blade. There are adjustments on all guards. If it's not lined up, boards can get hung up on the support right in the middle of making a cut.
- It's OK to just shave a little off from the end of a board. But avoid cut-offs that are shorter than 2 in. The blade will often catch them and send them flying.

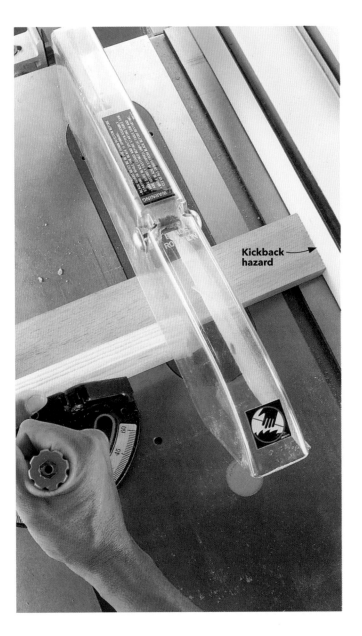

Kickback hazard

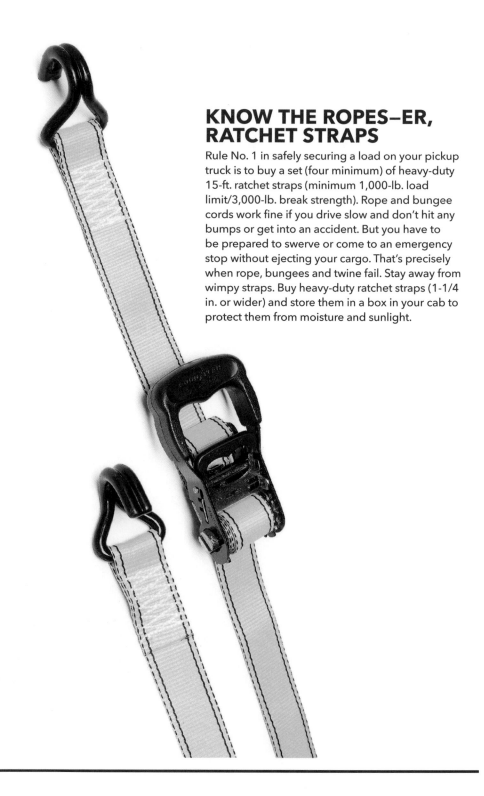

KNOW THE ROPES—ER, RATCHET STRAPS

Rule No. 1 in safely securing a load on your pickup truck is to buy a set (four minimum) of heavy-duty 15-ft. ratchet straps (minimum 1,000-lb. load limit/3,000-lb. break strength). Rope and bungee cords work fine if you drive slow and don't hit any bumps or get into an accident. But you have to be prepared to swerve or come to an emergency stop without ejecting your cargo. That's precisely when rope, bungees and twine fail. Stay away from wimpy straps. Buy heavy-duty ratchet straps (1-1/4 in. or wider) and store them in a box in your cab to protect them from moisture and sunlight.

Ice-Free Planks

Flip ladders and construction planks on their sides (or upside down) when storing them outdoors overnight in the winter. That will prevent ice from forming on the surface and keeps you safe the next day when want to use them.

Keep Your Cord Connections Dry

To avoid tripping ground fault circuit interrupters (GFCIs) when you're working outdoors in the winter, keep tool cord connections out of the mud and snow. To keep them high and dry, drill a hole near the bottom of your sawhorse and hook a carabiner into it. Secure the end of your extension cord with the carabiner and you're good to go.

USE A GFCI OUTDOORS

House chores—especially outdoors—often bring water and electricity together. The best way to make those situations safer is to use a GFCI. Newer homes have GFCI protection in bathroom, kitchen, garage and exterior outlets, but those GFCIs may no longer offer protection after 10 years or so. To be safe, plug your tools into a GFCI extension cord before you venture into the wet grass.

19 SECRET HIDING PLACES

Clever ways to hide your valuables

GOT SOME REAL valuables to hide? Frankly, the best advice is to get a safe-deposit box at your bank. But that's not very fun. Plus, it's a hassle if you need to get to your valuables often or quickly. Here are a bunch of clever, simple ways to hide those items from all but the smartest, most determined crooks.

2. AIR-RETURN STASH

Cut out a stud space opening to fit a return air grille. Cut off the grille screws and glue just the heads in place. Run four drywall screws into the corners of the opening so they fit just inside the rim of the grille. Then glue rare-earth magnets to the back of the grille so they line up with the screw heads.

1. RIGHT OUT IN THE OPEN

Vacuum cleaners, old printers, computer towers, children's toys. Any common household item that has a cavity will work. (Just be sure family members know about it so your valuables don't get donated or tossed!) For easy access, choose an item that opens instantly, such as a vacuum cleaner bag compartment. For more security, choose an item with a cover that screws shut.

3. BURIED TREASURE

Roll up some cash, stick it in a medicine bottle or any other watertight container, and bury it in a potted plant. For quicker access and to keep dirt from getting under your fingernails, place a stone or pine cone over it. Not many burglars are going to be excavating around your houseplants.

More Hiding Places

4. FALSE-BOTTOM DRAWER

Pick a deep drawer so the depth change won't be obvious. Cut 1/4-in. plywood 1/16 in. smaller than the drawer opening and rest it on a couple of wood strips that are hot-glued to the drawer sides. Then hot-glue some item you'd expect to find in that drawer to the bottom so you have a handle to lift the false bottom and reveal the booty.

5. CABINET HIDEY-HOLE

Between almost every pair of upper cabinets, there's a 1/2-in. gap. Take advantage of that gap by hanging a manila envelope containing, oh, I don't know, about two grand in hundred-dollar bills? Hang the cash with binder clips that are too wide to fall through the crack.

6. TOE-KICK HIDEAWAY

It takes carpentry skills, but you can pull off the toe-kicks under kitchen cabinets and make them removable. Most are 1/4-in. plywood held in place with 1-in. brads. If you have a secondary 3/4-in. toe-kick, you'll have to cut it out at both ends. An oscillating tool works well for that task.

Stick both halves of round hook-and-loop self-adhesive tape to the toe-kick. Then push the toe-kick into place. The adhesive will stick to the cabinet base and leave half of the hook-and-loop tape in place when you pull it free.

7. COUNTERFEIT CONTAINERS

Go online and type in "secret hiding places." You'll be amazed by how many brand-name phony containers are available. Comet, Coca-Cola, Bush's Beans—whatever. But you can craft a homemade version too. This mayonnaise jar interior was spray-painted with cream-colored paint for plastic.

8. THE APPLIANCE CAPER

If your refrigerator or dishwasher has a snap-off grille in the front, a lot of secret storage space is under there. Ask yourself this: How many burglars will be thinking about cleaning your refrigerator coils? But before you stuff treasures under a fridge, take a peek to see where the coils are. On some models, a stack of cash might block the airflow. That will make the fridge work harder and could even damage it.

FAMILY HANDYMAN'S FIELD EDITORS' SUGGESTIONS
Here are their favorite ideas for secret storage places:

9. "Drill a hole in the top of any interior door. Size it to fit a cylinder such as an old film container or a cigar tube. Roll up some bills and keep them there."

Note: If you want to do this trick on a hollow-core door, you have to stick close to the outside edges. Look at the door from the top and you'll see how wide the solid internal frame is.

10. "I put in a fake PVC pipe complete with a cleanout plug in my basement. Unscrew the plug and there are the goods."

11. "It took some effort, but I freed a tread from the oak stairs to my home's second story and attached a piano hinge to the back. It's almost invisible."

12. "Whenever I build a piece of furniture, I build in a stash spot. The last project I built was a dresser, and when I assembled it, I put a 1/4-in. sheet of plywood just above the top drawers and installed a piano hinge on the top. That's where we keep everything we care about."

13. "Believe it or not, I put our passports and a bit of cash underneath the shroud that covers the garage door opener."

14. "Which paint can contains the gold?"

15. "How many thieves are going to go through the dozens of pockets in your closet? I put cash in the pockets of my old pants and suit coats." Just be sure the clothes don't get donated!

16. "I think the key is to use lots of hiding places. It's stupid to put all your eggs in one basket. I keep hundred-dollar bills between pages in books, tape an envelope behind my headboard and put cash behind the false panel in my dishwasher."

17. "No burglar worth his salt looks in a kid's room for valuables. It's just full of useless junk. So find somewhere in there where the kid won't find it either."

18. "My secret stash is taped on the underside of drawers in the kitchen."

19. HIDE A KEY IN PLAIN SIGHT
Say you want to hide a key somewhere other than under the rug or over the door. Try mounting a phony plastic LB fitting. Screw it to the wall and run a bit of 1/2-in. conduit to the ground so it looks official. Cut the head off the bottom screw and glue it in place. Swing the cover aside and there's the key.

A BETTER PLACE TO AGE

Easy upgrades make home safer for older folks.

AS YOUR PARENTS or loved ones age, their homes may not age so well along with them. Older homes in particular can be challenging to navigate once decreased vision, mobility and strength, and other effects of aging, start to take a toll. Some home modifications, especially those designed to accommodate wheelchairs, can be expensive and complex. But many others are easy for most DIYers. Here are some simple ways to help keep parents and other loved ones living more comfortably in their own home and hopefully living longer, healthier lives as well.

Add Shower Grab Bars and Do the Yank Test

A securely fastened grab bar can be the difference between a momentary slip and a hip-breaking fall. The best location for grab bars depends on the needs of the person who'll be using them, so ask before you install them. General guidelines call for a vertical bar at the tub edge and an angled bar on the long back wall of the tub.

A 24-in. grab bar positioned at a 45-degree angle will attach easily to wall studs. If you can't anchor to a stud, you can secure wood blocking between the studs. You may be able to go through a closet or storage area behind the tub so the wall patch won't be highly visible, nor will it need to be perfect.

After you're done installing a grab bar, do the yank test by pulling on the bar with all your strength to make sure the bar will hold up when it's really needed. For detailed grab bar installation instructions, search "install grab bars" at *familyhandyman.com*.

Replace Toggle Switches with Rocker Switches

Rocker switches feature a big on/off plate that you can operate with a finger, a knuckle or even an elbow. Some rocker switches are illuminated to make them easy to find day or night. These great inventions use a tiny bit of electricity from the circuit they're on to light a small LED or neon bulb, and they install as easily as regular switches. For a selection of illuminated switches, go to *kyleswitchplates.com*.

Extend Stair Rails

The handrails for exterior stairs typically end at the bottom step. But stepping off the bottom step (or preparing to step up on it) is actually when someone is the most off balance and likely to fall. Simple Rail handrail kits from Simplified Building make it easy for DIYers to build an extended handrail that fits any stairway. The kits use Kee Klamp pipe fittings and come with all the components you need (such as fittings, pipe, connectors and railings) at reasonable prices. Visit *simplifiedbuilding.com* to see exactly what you need to accomplish your project.

Install Low-Pile Carpet

Thick carpet pile over a thick pad is the worst for anyone who is unstable when walking—it increases the likelihood of tripping and falling. It's also more difficult for pushing and maneuvering wheelchairs and walkers. To make getting around easier, consider installing a low-profile commercial-grade level loop or cut pile carpet with a pile height of no more than 1/2 in. and a 1/4-in. (10-lb. density) pad.

Raise Your Washer and Dryer

To make it easier on aging backs and knees, set your front-loading washing machines and dryers on pedestals 12 to 15 in. above the floor. To find out how to build a simple washer/dryer pedestal, visit familyhandyman.com and search "DIY washer pedestal."

Replace Cabinet Knobs with Handles

Arthritis and stiff joints make grabbing small round knobs on cabinet drawers and doors difficult. Replace them with C- or D-shaped pulls, which let you tuck your fingers around them, making it easier to open the door or drawer. Consider this for your own kitchen too. Adding new pulls and handles is a quick, inexpensive way to update a kitchen while making it more comfortable and convenient to use over the long term.

Install "Invisible" Grab Bars

Sometimes people are reluctant to add grab bars because they think it will make their home look institutional. But stylish and sturdy grab bars come in many shapes, sizes and finishes, and some, such as those in the elegant Invisia Collection, serve double duty as towel racks, toilet paper holders, corner shelves and more. Search in your browser for online sources for "designer grab bars" and "specialty grab bars."

Widen Doorways with Offset Hinges

Navigating narrow doorways is tough for someone using a wheelchair or walker. Doorways can be widened, but it's a complex and costly job. An easier solution is to replace the existing hinges with expandable offset door hinges. These special hinges are designed to swing the door clear of the opening and add 2 in. of clearance. The hinge measures 2 in. x 3-1/2 in. and wraps around the door trim. You need at least 3 in. between the inside of the doorjamb and the adjoining wall for the hinges to fit. They use the existing holes and screws and come in a variety of finishes. Offset hinges are sold online and at many home centers.

Remodel with Aging in Mind

A kitchen remodel is the perfect opportunity to build in universal design components that will look great and allow the room to work well as you age in your own home. Consider incorporating:

- Rollout drawers and pull-down shelf inserts
- Appliances with touchpad controls instead of knobs
- A shallow (6-in.-deep) sink, which is easier to use than a deep one
- Countertops at different levels so someone seated can work comfortably
- A side-by-side refrigerator with a long, continuous handle that someone who is seated can easily open
- Under-cabinet task lighting
- Drawer storage rather than upper cabinetry

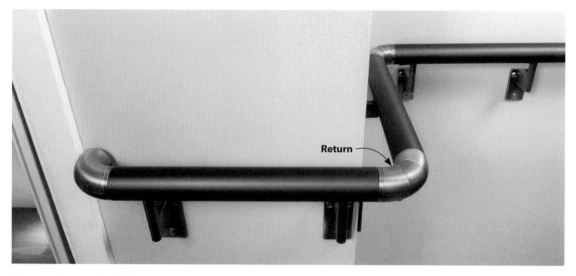

Return

Install Handrails in Hallways

Long hallways can be tough on people with limited mobility, which is the reason so many senior care centers have continuous handrail systems. Consider adding the same safety feature at home. You can install a simple wooden railing or consider the Promenaid handrail system, a problem-solving product with a unique bracket that slides along an open channel in the bottom of the handrail. This lets you locate the handrail anywhere and slide the brackets to wherever studs are located without adding extra blocking. The brackets also pivot so you can install the handrail vertically or at an angle. These elegant handrails have snap-on end caps and returns, and the articulating joints allow them to go around corners or along stairs. You can buy complete kits or individual components at *promenaid.com*. Just make sure any handrail you install has returns.

A Showerhead Grab Bar Is a Big Help

For people with limited mobility or who prefer to shower while seated, a handheld showerhead is a terrific help. And even better is a handheld showerhead on a sliding rail that allows for individual adjustment. But because those rails are often flimsy, grabbing one could be a disaster. Delta's adjustable slide bar/grab bar hand shower is the best of both worlds. It's an ADA-compliant grab bar with a sliding handheld showerhead in one attractive package.

Light Up a Keyhole

It's no fun to fumble for your keys, but for people with diminished sight, finding a keyhole at night is extremely difficult. And there's an element of added safety when you can unlock and enter your home at night without delay. If you can, mount a motion-activated light above the keyhole or on a wall just to the side; it will turn on automatically when you reach to put your key in the lock. Alternatively, keep a handheld flashlight with your keys to easily illuminate the lock.

Add a Rolling Cart to the Kitchen

A rolling cart is helpful in any kitchen, but it's especially helpful for older cooks. It's a convenient prep center, and models with drawers or shelves allow someone to store frequently used items and roll it around so their tools are always close at hand. And it can be extremely useful for someone who has diminished strength or dexterity to ferry items to and from the table without the risk of dropping things or injuring themselves.

Add Grab Bars Near Exterior Doors

Grab bars aren't just helpful in the bathroom; they're also useful near exterior doors, inside and out. For people who are unsteady on their feet, the simple act of opening a door can be difficult. A grab bar gives them something solid to hang on to near house and garage entrances and steps. For maximum installation options, choose a bar that can be mounted horizontally, vertically or diagonally.

Replace Doorknobs

Gripping and twisting a doorknob can be hard for people with arthritis or a loss of dexterity. Lever handles solve that problem. Simply press down on the lever to release the door latch without gripping anything. In fact, an elbow or forearm works too. Many lever handles are reversible, which means they'll fit either a right-handed or left-handed door. (Handedness is determined by which side the door hinges are on when you stand outside the door as it swings away from you into the room.) But check the handle requirements before you buy so you get the right handle for your situation.

Put a Bench Near Steps

This allows people to steady themselves after they climb up or down. It's also a good idea to set a chair at the end of a long hallway for resting. Just make sure it's placed so that it's not a tripping hazard.

CHAPTER 5

EVERYDAY SOLUTIONS

KEEP PICTURES LEVEL

A pinch of mounting putty (the sticky stuff used to hang posters) keeps pictures level without damaging walls.

Cosmetic Touch-Up Tool

Disposable cosmetics applicators (sold at drugstores) are great for small touch-up jobs. They let you put a dab of paint or finish precisely where you want it. No mess, and no brushes to clean up.

Flash Find

If you lose a contact lens, turn off the lights and shine a flashlight
beam across the floor. The lens will glimmer and make it an easy find.

3/4" PVC
fitting

LED puck
light

Not connected
to power

WIRELESS WALL SCONCE

You can add a wall sconce to a hallway or other location without having to tear open a wall to run the electrical cable and add a switch. Just install this wireless version that looks like the real deal. Mount a sconce to the wall and glue a puck light to a 3/4-in. male threaded PVC fitting. Then screw the fitting into the lightbulb socket. These puck lights are battery powered and include a remote control switch.

Block
for
higher
doors

Pry bar

USE A PRY BAR AS A LEVER

Use a lever and fulcrum to ease the awkwardness of hanging a door by yourself. Hang doors back onto hinges by levering the door into position with a pry bar as a fulcrum on a 3/4-in. block of wood. Line up the top hinge leaves, slip in the top hinge pin and then line up the other leaves and drop in the other pins.

Unpeel Peel-and-Stick

Separating contact paper from its backing can be a frustrating endeavor. To solve the problem, put a piece of tape on one corner of the contact paper and another piece on the same corner of the backing. Fold down the top of each piece of tape about 1/2 in. to get a better grip, and then pull apart the pieces of tape. The paper and backing should separate easily. This also works well on labels, stickers and the like.

Fix for Sagging Shelves

Here's a clever way to keep shelves from sagging. Cut a piece of plywood the height of the space between the shelves and just wide enough to provide support for the shelf. Cut enough pages out of an unwanted book to accommodate the plywood brace. Glue the plywood into the book and tuck it in with your other books, near the center of the shelf.

Shelf support

A STURDIER GROCERY BAG

Cloth grocery bags make a lot of sense—except for the flimsy piece of plastic that's often found at the bottom of the bag. Replace it with something that will hold up much better: a piece of pegboard. Cut it to size and slip it into the bottom. You'll find the pegboard is lightweight and the holes help keep the bags dry. The reworked bag can hold heavier items and it's easier to pack.

GENTLE HANDCART

A handcart is great for moving furniture. To upgrade it and protect pieces with delicate finishes, cover the sides and top with pipe insulation. Secure it with duct tape.

Folded Sanding Pad

What's the best power sander in your shop? A quarter sheet of sandpaper and your bare hand! To improve the longevity of this natural marvel, apply spray adhesive to the quarter sheets, then fold them over to make a double-thick one-eighth sheet. They work great for sanding sculpted and molded edges, and the double-ply thickness lets you press hard without tearing a hole in the paper.

Clamp a Nail

When there's no room for a hammer, sink the nail with a C-clamp. This trick works for plumbing and electrical straps, junction boxes and even joist hangers.

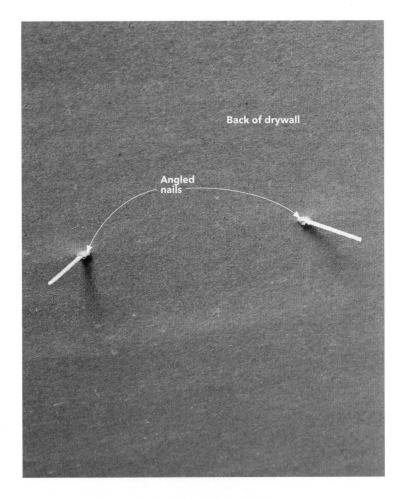

Back of drywall

Angled
nails

NO STUD? NO PROBLEM!

Studs aren't always located where you need them. When you need
to nail trim where there's no stud, dab some construction adhesive on
the back of the trim and then drive nails into the drywall at 45-degree
angles. That holds the trim tight against the wall while the adhesive
cures. This "trap nailing" technique works fine with brad nailers and
even better with finish nailers.

Notched
paint stick

SUPER PAINT SCRAPER

When you're pouring paint from a gallon paint
can, a lot of paint clings to the can's walls. To get
all the paint, cut a notch in the handle end of a
wood paint stick. Now you can scrape the inside
of the can clean and use every last drop.

Low-expansion foam

Stiffen a Shower Arm

Here's a quick way to make a loose shower arm stay put: Pull the escutcheon plate away from the wall. Mask around the arm and surrounding area to prevent a mess. Then shoot in a little expanding foam sealant. Use a low-expansion foam and inject just enough foam to fill in around the arm.

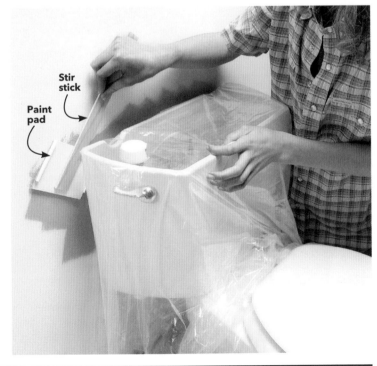

Stir stick

Paint pad

Paint Pad for Tight Spots

If you have a tight spot to paint, try this method: Remove the pad from a paint edging tool (sold at paint stores and home centers) and hot-glue the pad to a stir stick. Now you've got a painting tool that will fit behind toilet tanks and radiators.

Water Spout Extender

When filling a water bottle at your refrigerator's water dispenser, you practically have to get on your knees and tilt your head to see exactly where the water will dispense. To avoid that, cut a small section from a silicone straw (other tubing would work too) and put it on the dispenser so you can see where the water will come out. Now you can fill your water bottles without having to do yoga poses.

Silicone straw

Fresh Tape

Sometimes, masking tape that's been sitting on a shelf for years won't pull off the roll without tearing. Freshen it by microwaving it for 10 seconds. Heat softens the adhesive for easy release.

**A/C
condensate
line**

A/C WATER FOR
THE GARDEN

You may be sending tons of water from your A/C
condensate down the drain. Why not put the water
to use? You can disconnect the condensate line
and redirect the drain to empty into a 5-gal. bucket.
Leave the original drain line in place so at the end of
the cooling season, or if you're away for more than
a day, you can reconnect the drain. You could divert
thousands of gallons of free water from your air
conditioner for use on plants and in the garden.

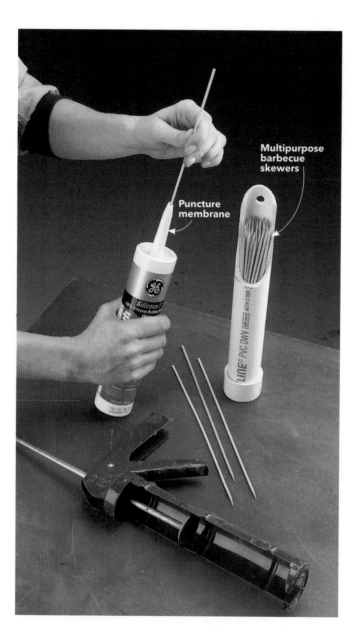

Multipurpose barbecue skewers

Puncture membrane

MULTI-SKILLED SKEWERS

Pick up a pack of wood skewers (sold at grocery stores) for barbecuing and keep them handy in your shop. Here are some great uses for them:

- Puncture that pesky seal in caulk tubes.
- Apply glue in dowel holes or biscuit slots.
- Scrape gunk out of crevices on furniture you're refinishing.
- Plug any stripped-out screw holes on antique furniture so that the screws will grip tightly.

Make Plastic Fittings Actually Fit

The most common complaint about shop vacuum fittings is that they don't always fit the tools that need them. Softening plastic fittings with a heat gun can help make these mismatched pieces play nice with each other.

Safe Blade Storage

To keep reciprocating saw and jigsaw blades sharp, safe and handy, use travel toothbrush holders. Keep similar blades in each holder and mark the blade type with a permanent marker. The holders work great for blades 6 in. and smaller.

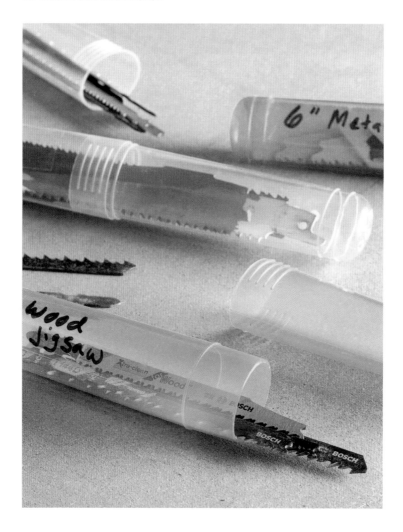

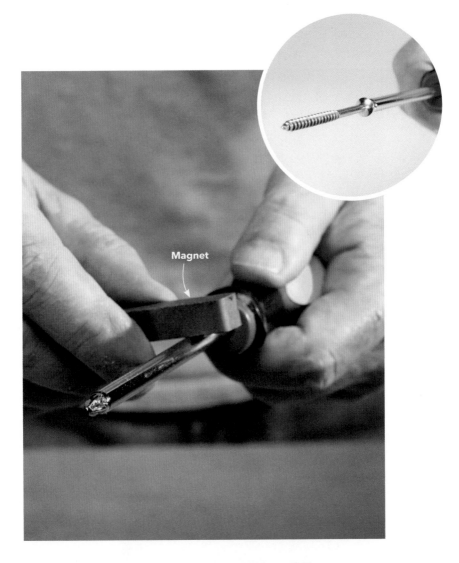

Magnet

MAGNETIZE A SCREWDRIVER

This trick could save you hundreds of dropped screws over your DIY lifetime. Grab a magnet and rub it along the shaft of a screwdriver a dozen times or so. Rub in one direction only, kind of like you would do to sharpen a knife. In about 10 seconds, you'll have a magnetic screwdriver. Repeat as needed.

Metal strip

Bend and bolt on end

GETTING AN EDGE ON PAINT STRIPPING

Here's an idea for making paint stripping faster and easier. Cut two slots directly across from each other in the rim of a 3-lb. coffee can (a Dremel rotary tool with a cutoff wheel works great to cut the slots). Drop a 1/16-in.-thick metal strip (sold at home centers and hardware stores) in the slots, folding and bolting the metal strip to the can. Now you can work swiftly and cleanly while stripping, loading up a 4-in.-wide drywall knife and scraping it against the metal edge to clean the sludge off the blade for another pass.

Flip-up Downspout

Pulling off downspout extensions and jamming them back on is a nuisance when you're mowing. But you can convert all your extensions to flip-up versions in about an hour with inexpensive hardware. Make a 1/2-in.-deep cut across the extension about 3 in. from the end with a hacksaw. Then use metal snips to finish cutting out a notch. Fasten the extension to the downspout with sheet metal screws or 1/8-in. aluminum rivets. For smooth operation, place plastic fender washers between the two parts. Make sure the extension hangs about 1/2 in. below the downspout.

Plastic washer

1/2" space

1/2"

No-Sweat Fence Post Pulling

To remove a stubborn 4x4 fence post, fasten a 2x4 to the post with five or six screws. Then just set a car jack on a board or a block underneath the 2x4 and jack the post right out of the hole.

2x4

Flat surface for jack

NONSTICK MOWER DECK

If the underside of your lawn mower develops a thick crust of grass clippings, scrub it clean and then give it a coat of spray lubricant. Products that contain silicone or Teflon work best and can be purchased at home centers and hardware stores.

EASY-FLIP BURGERS

Run a cut onion across the grate of your barbecue grill. The natural anticoagulant in the onion makes the surface less sticky for meats, so your burgers will be easy to flip.

KILL CRABGRASS NOW!

The most cost-effective way to control crabgrass is to use a fertilizer with crabgrass preventer added to it. But you have to do this in the spring before crabgrass seeds germinate. Apply it between the second and third times you mow, and do it just before it rains to work both the fertilizer and the herbicide into the soil. The fertilizer will help thicken the turf. Thicker turf helps squeeze out crabgrass plants missed by the herbicide.

Easy Ice Scraping

Sick of freezing your tail off while you're scraping the rock-hard ice off your windshield? Try this cool tip. Just mix two parts water with one part isopropyl (rubbing) alcohol in a spray bottle and spray it on your windshield. The ice will melt almost instantly. The alcohol won't harm your car's paint, but it will remove car wax, so try to keep it off waxed surfaces. To prevent ice buildup, try Prestone Ice & Frost Shield. "You spray it on before heading in for the night or when you arrive at work," says automotive expert Rick Muscoplat. "Any snow or freezing rain won't stick to your windshield. I gave it to my daughter and she uses it when she arrives at work. If it snows during the day, she just has to turn on the wipers and go."

Don't Lose Your Tools

It's not a big deal when a tool falls out of your pouch—unless you don't know it fell out, and it's snowing. Give yourself a fighting chance to find misplaced hand tools by marking them with a bright-colored spray paint. This is also a good way to identify your tools so they don't wander off with other workers.

Speed square

GUTTER DECK PLANTER

Cut a 2-ft. length of vinyl gutter and glue one of the end caps into place with kitchen and bath adhesive caulk. Drill 1/2-in. drainage holes every 4 in. along the bottom of the gutter. Slide both fascia support brackets onto the gutter and glue the other end cap into place. Screw the planter to the deck rail through the fascia support brackets using galvanized screws.

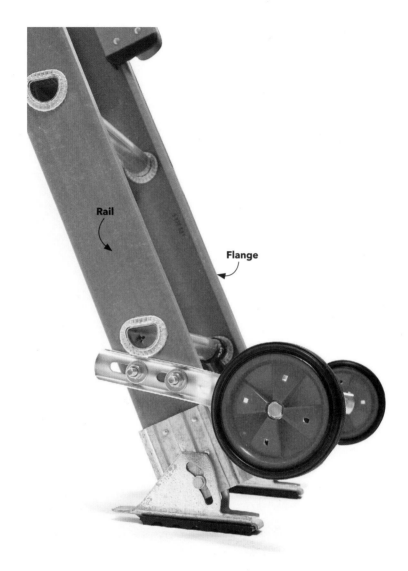

Rail

Flange

ROLLING LADDER

Encourage your kids to master bicycle balance fast, because here's
a great use for training wheels: Drill holes in your extension ladder
and bolt on the wheels for easy mobility. Just be sure to position
the wheels so they lift well off the ground when you stand the ladder
up. Use bolts no larger than 1/4 in. in diameter. Drill holes only in
the sides of the rails at least 1/2 in. from the flanges.

Handy Soil Sifter

A large plastic milk crate with a grid-work bottom makes a great soil sifter. Weeds, roots and rocks stay in the crate. If the holes are too big to sift out the material, you can line the crate with 1/2-in. or 1/4-in. hardware cloth.

Closing the Gap

Keep mulch from clogging the tailgate opening of your truck. Use a PVC pipe to fill the gap. When not using the pipe, you can store it behind the front seat.

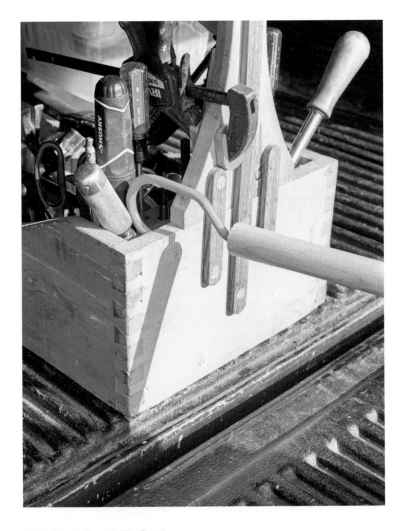

CARGO HOOK

Packing and unpacking a truck with a tonneau cover in place can be a pain. To make it easier, put a utility hook on the end of a broom handle. You can just push things in with the handle and retrieve them with the hook.

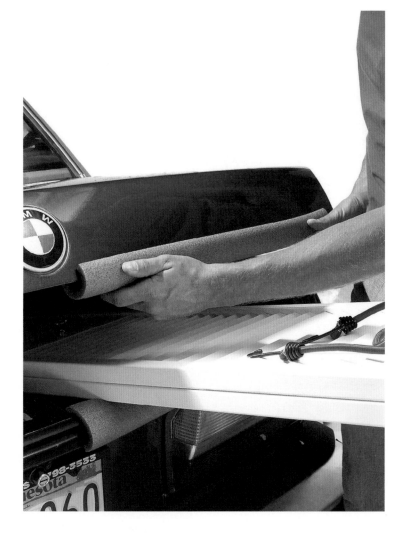

TRUNK BUMPERS

Keep a couple of sections of 3/4-in. pipe insulation in your trunk to protect both the car's paint and your oversized cargo. A package of pipe insulation is inexpensive at home centers and hardware stores.

HANG IT STRAIGHT, LEVEL & SOLID

With these three techniques, you can hang just about anything on your walls, and keep it there

Hang Pictures Straight & Level

THE FIRST CHALLENGE in hanging a picture is deciding exactly where you want it. It's not so hard with just one picture. You can ask a helper to hold it up while you stand back and judge the position.

Most experts recommend hanging a picture with its center about 60 in. from the floor, or bottom

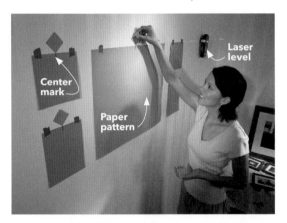

1 Project a level line and tape exact-size paper patterns on the wall. Mark the top center of each pattern with the corner of a sticky note.

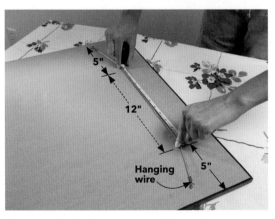

2 Stretch the hanger wire with two fingers spaced equally distant from the edges of the picture frame. Keep the wire parallel to the top of the frame. Measure the distance between your fingertips.

edge 6 to 8 in. above a piece of furniture. Use these heights as a starting point. Then adjust the position of the picture to your liking, and mark the top center with the corner of a sticky note. Use the technique in **Photos 2-6** to complete the job.

A group of pictures is trickier. First cut out paper patterns and arrange them on the wall with low-adhesive masking tape. The temporary red line from a laser level is helpful for aligning a series of photos level with one another **(Photo 1)**. The laser level is ideal because you get a perfectly straight line without having to mark up the walls. A standard carpenter's level will also work.

When you arrive at a grouping that's pleasing, mark the top center of each pattern with the corner of a sticky note **(Photo 1)**. You'll use the bottom corner of each sticky note as a reference point for locating the picture hangers.

Now you're ready to position the picture hangers **(Photos 2-4)**. Use two hangers for each picture as extra support and to help keep the picture from tipping. Choose picture hangers that are rated to support the weight of your art. We recommend professional hangers such as the one shown below. They work fine in drywall. These are available at home centers or from most picture-framing shops. OOK is one popular brand. Plaster may not support pictures as well as drywall does. To hang heavier art on plaster walls, use picture hangers with double or triple nails.

Photos 2 and 3 show how to measure the space between the hangers and the distance from the top of the picture frame. The distance between hangers isn't critical. Just space your fingers several inches from the outside edges of the picture frame. Transfer these measurements to the wall **(Photo 4)**. An inexpensive level with inches marked along the edge is a great picture-hanging tool **(Photo 4)**. Otherwise, just stick masking tape to the edge of a level and transfer measurements to the tape. Then line up the bottom of the hooks with the marks and drive the picture-hanger nails through the angled guides on the hooks **(Photo 5)**.

3 Leave one finger in place and measure the distance from the wire to the top. Use this dimension and the dimension from **Photo 2** to position the picture hangers.

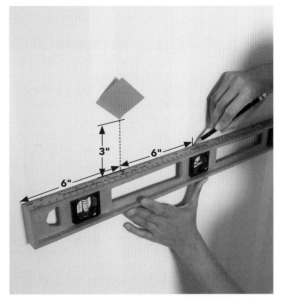

4 Find the hanger positions by measuring down from the sticky note and to each side from center. Keep the hangers level.

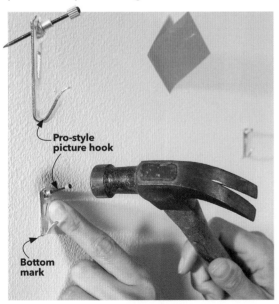

Pro-style picture hook

Bottom mark

5 Align the bottom edge of a picture hook with the mark and then drive a nail through the hook's guide.

6 Slip the wire over both hooks. Slide the picture sideways across the wires until it's level. Use the same process to hang the remaining pictures.

Hang Heavy Mirrors with Confidence

TAKE EXTRA PRECAUTIONS when you're hanging a heavy mirror. If the mirror has a hanging wire on the back, remove it and instead screw D-rings to the frame **(Photo 1)**. (Mirrors without frames should be hung with special mirror hangers.) Install the D-rings an equal distance from the top of the frame, about one-third of the total height down. Then measure the exact distance between the centers of the D-rings **(Photo 1)**. The trick is to hook your tape measure on one edge of a D-ring and measure to the same edge of the second D-ring. Record this measurement. Then measure down to the top of the D-rings **(Photo 2)**.

Photo 3 shows how to transfer the measurements to the wall. But first you'll have to hold the mirror up to the wall and choose the best position. Start with the center of the mirror at about 60 in. from the floor. When you like the position, mark the top center with a sticky note.

Some picture hangers are rated to support heavy mirrors, but it's safer to install hollow-wall anchors instead, which are stronger. We recommend the screw-in type of anchor shown below. It's rated to support 40 lbs.

Weigh your mirror and choose the appropriate type of anchor. Use toggle-type anchors **(Photo 3)** for heavier mirrors. Measure from your reference point to position the anchors **(Photo 3)**. Make starter holes with an awl or Phillips screwdriver. If you hit a stud with the awl, simply drive a screw.

Photo 5 shows how to hang the mirror. If the top isn't level when you're done, wrap a few turns of electrical tape around the D-ring on the low side to raise that side slightly.

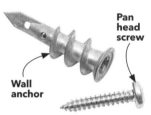

Pan head screw

Wall anchor

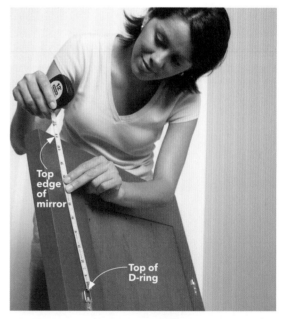

Right edge

D-ring

Right edge

Mirror back

Top edge of mirror

Top of D-ring

1 Measure from the right edge of one D-ring to the right edge of the other D-ring for the distance between the centers of the hanging D-rings.

2 Measure from the top of the D-ring to the top of the frame to determine the distance down.

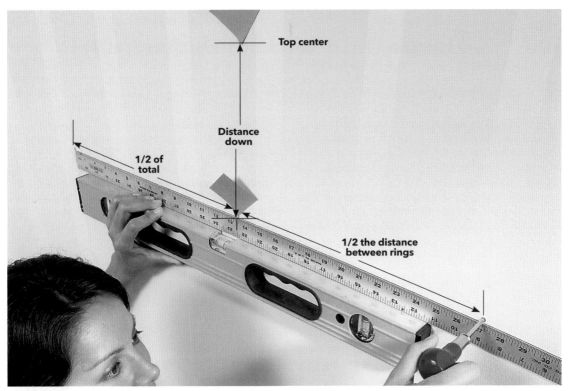

3 Use a level and a ruler to plumb down the correct distance. Mark the spot with the corner of a sticky note. Then use the level and ruler to find the exact hanger positions.

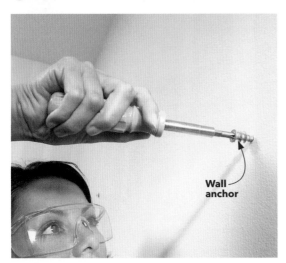

4 Drive a wall anchor into the drywall at each hook location.

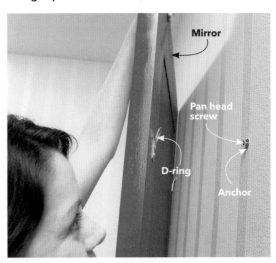

5 Screw a pan head screw into the anchor. Leave the screw sticking out about 1/4 in. Hook the D-rings onto the protruding screws.

Hang a Quilt Without Damaging It

ONE GOOD WAY to display a quilt is to hang it on a wall. But don't just tack it up by the corners or it'll stretch out of shape. Instead, use this method for quilts or other decorative textiles because it distributes the weight for smooth hanging and minimal stress to the fabric. The hand stitching **(Photo 1)** doesn't damage the quilt—it only goes through the backing, and it's easy to remove when you no longer wish to display the quilt.

Measure the top edge of the quilt and purchase the same lengths of 1-1/2-in.-wide sew-on hook-and-loop fastener strip and 2-1/2-in.-wide cotton or synthetic webbing. We found the hook-and-loop strip at a fabric store and the webbing at an upholsterer's shop. You'll also need a length of 1-1/2-in.-wide pine or poplar, a staple gun and several 2-1/2-in. wood screws.

Photos 1–3 show how to prepare and hang the quilt. If the quilt pattern allows, it's best to rotate the quilt 180 degrees every month or so. This relieves stress on the fabric and helps prevent uneven fading. To be able to rotate the quilt, you'll have to sew another strip of hook-and-loop along the opposite edge.

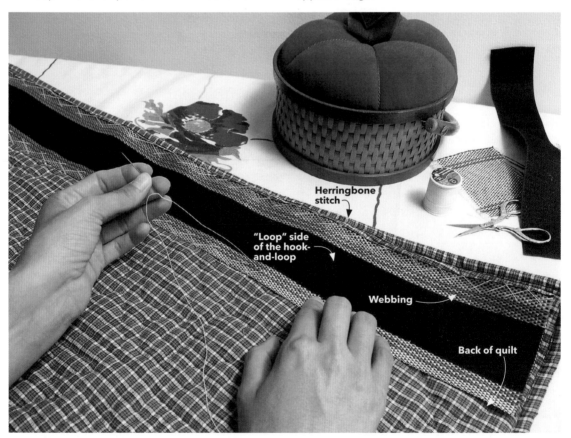

Herringbone stitch

"Loop" side of the hook-and-loop

Webbing

Back of quilt

1 Sew the loop side of the hook-and-loop to the webbing. Then stitch the webbing to the back of the quilt using a herringbone stitch as shown.

Stud
location

"Hook" side
of hook-
and-loop

2-1/2"
screw

1/4"
staple

3/4" x 1-1/2"
wood strip

2 Staple the hook side of the hook-and-loop to the wood strip. Determine the best position, and level the wood strip and screw it to the studs.

3 Hang the quilt by smoothing the hook-and-loop tape that's sewn on the back of the quilt along the tape stapled to the wood strip.

SAVE YOUR FURNITURE

Easy repairs for chairs, shelves and more

THE CREAKING SOUND you hear each time you sit on that old kitchen chair is not a good sign. It has loose joints, and every time you sit on it, you're wearing them down and further loosening them. Someday it's going to fall apart.

One of these tips will save that chair—and many other pieces of your favorite furniture, too. But keep in mind that these are fast, easy and practical fixes. They are not the best repairs for treasured heirlooms or valuable antiques.

Add Braces

Chair braces are an easy fix for a wobbly chair. They're better looking and much stiffer than L-brackets (see "Add Metal Braces"). Most hardware stores carry inexpensive chair braces in finishes such as chrome, brass or bronze. To avoid splitting the wood, be sure to drill 1/8-in. pilot holes before driving in the screws.

Glide

Fix a Wobbly Table

If you've got a table that rocks on an uneven floor, you've probably tried wedging something under the short leg. It doesn't last, does it? Here's a better way: Use washers and nail-on glides.

First, drill holes for the nails with a 1/16-in. bit and install the glides. Then set the table in place and slip washers under the low leg until the table is steady. When you have determined how many washers are needed, pull off the glide and reinstall it, along with the washers.

Backer

3/4" hole

Rescue a Drawer

Drawer fronts that are just nailed or stapled to the drawer box often come loose or even fall off completely. You could simply pound the parts back together, but that kind of fix won't last long. For a repair that's stronger than the original construction, add a backer to the drawer front.

Make the backer from 3/4-in. plywood. Cut it to fit tight inside the drawer. With a spade bit, drill 3/4-in.-diameter holes in the plywood so you can access the screws that hold the drawer's handle. Fasten the backer to the inside front of the drawer, then screw the drawer sides to the ends of the backer.

Support Sagging Shelves

If your shelves sag, sometimes you can simply flip them over–but eventually they'll droop again. Here's a permanent solution: Add supports that fit tightly between the shelves.

Pine stair tread, which has a rounded front edge, is perfect for this. It's available at all home stores and is inexpensive. Many stores will cut it to length for you. You can paint or stain the supports to match the shelves, of course. But if the shelves hold books, consider staining them a color similar to your books. You'll be surprised at how well the supports blend in.

Dowel

Inject Epoxy Into Loose Joints

When one or two joints loosen on a chair but you can't get the rest of them apart, here's an advanced repair technique to try: Inject epoxy into the loose joints using a syringe.

Once mixed, most epoxy is too thick to push through a syringe. However, an epoxy used for fiberglass boat repair (such as the one shown here) has just the right consistency. To inject the glue, drill 1/8-in. holes in an inconspicuous place in line with the dowels. Aim for the cavity behind each dowel. Insert the syringe into the hole, then inject the epoxy until it runs out of the joint. Push the joint together, then wipe off the excess epoxy.

West System 101-TS packets are convenient for storing and dispensing epoxy. They're like ketchup packages–you just tear off the top and squeeze. They're available online (one source is *westmarine.com*), but this epoxy is more expensive than the hardware store variety. Plastic syringes are available at many pharmacies and online.

Save It With Screws

When ready-to-assemble (RTA) particleboard furniture breaks, the original knockdown fasteners often pull out of the wood and can't be replaced. The solution is to bypass them completely and screw the piece together from the outside.

Ordinary screws won't hold in particleboard, however. You need 2-1/2-in. to 3-in. screws with coarse threads and large, washer-style heads. (Large heads prevent the screws from being pulled through the particleboard.) Many home centers carry cabinet installation screws that are perfect for the job. Be sure to drill a pilot hole first, even if the screws have self-tapping points. You can also buy colored self-stick caps to cover the screw heads.

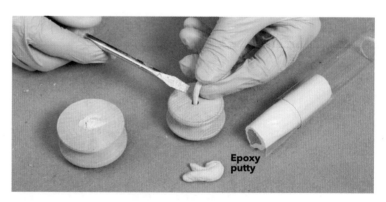

Epoxy putty

Fill Stripped-Out Screw Holes

Wooden drawer knobs tend to strip out and then come loose or even pull off. Using a fatter screw or shoving matchsticks into the hole might work, but here's a sure fix: Fill the hole with epoxy putty, then drill a new hole. Epoxy putty is available at home centers and hardware stores.

Epoxy putty is easy to use. You just cut off the amount you want, knead the piece until the inner and outer layers blend together, then roll it between your fingers to form a thin string. Push the string of putty into the hole with a screwdriver. Then scrape off the excess before it hardens.

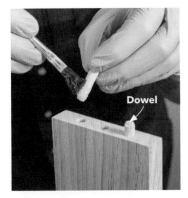

Dowel

Strengthen Ready-to-Assemble Furniture

New furniture that's put together with bolts and nuts often loosens up with use. You can take the piece apart and strengthen it with epoxy.

Most ready-to-assemble furniture uses loose-fitting dowels to align each part. Spread epoxy inside the dowel holes and on the dowels themselves when you reassemble the piece. (If the dowels fit nice and tight, use yellow glue instead—it's more convenient.) Don't spread glue on the ends of each part. They usually butt up against a finished surface, and no glue will stick to a finish for very long.

Add Metal Braces

If appearance doesn't matter, screwing a brace or T-plate onto a piece of furniture is often the quickest way to fix it. Adding metal may not make the piece totally sound, but at least it won't come apart.

Shim

Shim a Hinge

When a door won't close or align with a catch, placing a shim behind one of its hinges might solve the problem. The shim will kick out the upper or lower half of the door, depending on which hinge you choose.

Make the shim from one or more playing cards. Remove the hinge, and then cut the cards to fit into the hinge's recess. Place each piece in the recess and punch screw holes in it using an awl or a small Phillips screwdriver. Remount the hinge with the original screws.

CHAPTER 6

TOOLS & TECHNIQUES

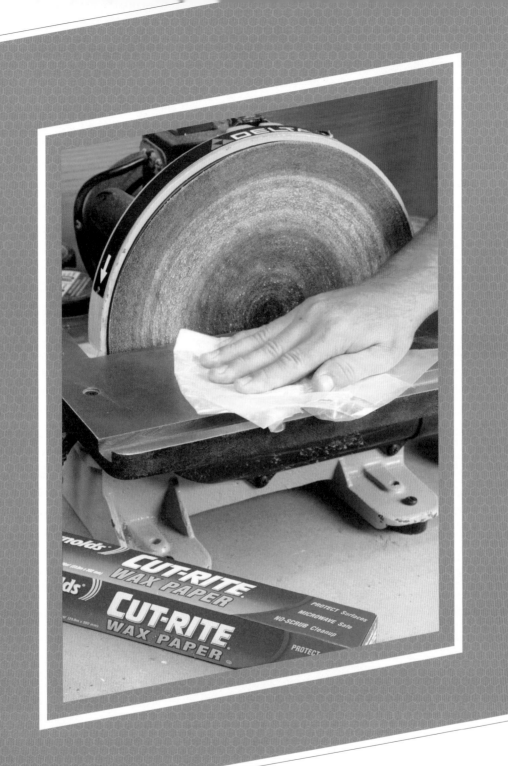

FISHING FOR POSITION

Here's a foolproof way to position holes when you run wires from your basement to the main floor: Set a large aquarium-cleaning magnet (sold at pet stores) on the main floor, then have a helper find it from below with the other magnet. After the magnets connect between the floors, drag them slowly to the location where you want the hole.

Living Room–Friendly Miter Saw

Running a miter saw in the house is a bad idea—it blows dust all over. But running to the shop for each cut doesn't make sense either. So, here's a simple "miter box" for a pull saw. First, make accurate 45- and 90-degree cuts on a 2x4 using a miter saw. Then, glue and nail these pieces to a scrap of plywood, using the saw's blade as a spacer. Now just clamp the miter box to a sawhorse right in the room where you're working and make your cuts. No airborne dust, and no running back and forth to the shop!

Use an Auxiliary Handle

Although you'll often use a hole saw in a handheld drill, sawing large holes is a tough job, so use your most powerful drill. Besides power, the drill should have an auxiliary handle, as hole saws don't act like drill bits. They have a tendency to "catch," giving your wrist a nasty twist. It can even yank the drill right out of your hand while the spinning drill handle crashes into anything in its path. An auxiliary handle lessens the chance of losing your grip.

Auxiliary handle

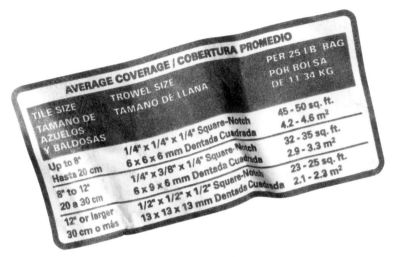

AVERAGE COVERAGE / COBERTURA PROMEDIO		PER 25 LB BAG POR BOLSA DE 11.34 KG
TILE SIZE TAMANO DE AZUELOS Y BALDOSAS	TROWEL SIZE TAMANO DE LLANA	
Up to 8" Hasta 20 cm	1/4" x 1/4" x 1/4" Square-Notch 6 x 6 x 6 mm Dentada Cuadrada	45 - 50 sq. ft. 4.2 - 4.6 m²
8" to 12" 20 a 30 cm	1/4" x 3/8" x 1/4" Square-Notch 6 x 9 x 6 mm Dentada Cuadrada	32 - 35 sq. ft. 2.9 - 3.3 m²
12" or larger 30 cm o más	1/2" x 1/2" x 1/2" Square-Notch 13 x 13 x 13 mm Dentada Cuadrada	23 - 25 sq. ft. 2.1 - 2.3 m²

DON'T TRUST THIS LABEL!

If you have a package of thin-set mortar, it probably has a chart like this one on the label. Don't rely on it. The recommendations are a good starting point, but they don't guarantee you'll have enough for the job. Buy a little more thin-set than you think you'll need. It's better to have some left over than not enough!

SCRAPE AWAY CEILING TEXTURE FOR A NEATER PAINT JOB

A neat, straight paint line at the top of a wall is tough to achieve next to a bumpy ceiling. So before you paint the wall, drag a narrow flat-head screwdriver lightly along the ceiling. You'll get a clean paint line and no one will ever notice that the bumps are missing.

PIPE-FINDING PRESCRIPTION

A stethoscope (sold at drugstores) lets you locate plumbing lines inside walls when you're planning a remodeling project. You need a steady flow of water, so turn on faucets full blast to find supply lines. To locate waste lines, have a helper flush toilets or fill sinks and let them drain. You'll hear the flow from several feet away, and the sound will get noticeably louder as you get closer. You'll be able to locate pipes within a foot or so. A stethoscope also lets you hear the hiss of larger leaks in supply lines.

Hang Crown Molding by Yourself

Hanging long pieces of crown molding can be difficult without a helper. Here's a trick that works: A removable utility wall hook such as 3M's Command will help support one end of the crown molding while you start nailing the other.

Pull the adhesive strip down when you're done

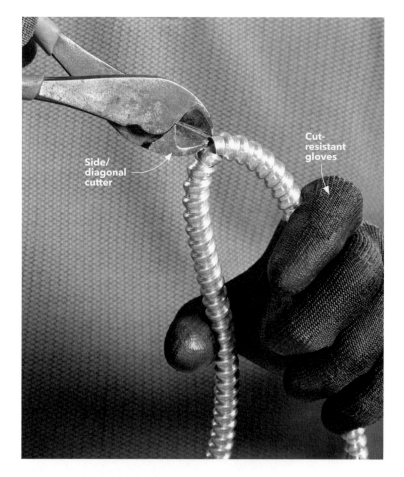

Side/
diagonal
cutter

Cut-
resistant
gloves

Bend and Cut

If you just have one or two cuts to make in MC cable and don't want
to invest in a cutting tool, bend the cable sharply until the armor pops
open, and then use that opening to start the cut with a side/diagonal
cutter. You only need to cut through one section in the armor. This
method will leave a jagged edge that will need to be trimmed after
the armor is separated. The cut ends of MC cable are sharp, so be
sure to wear gloves.

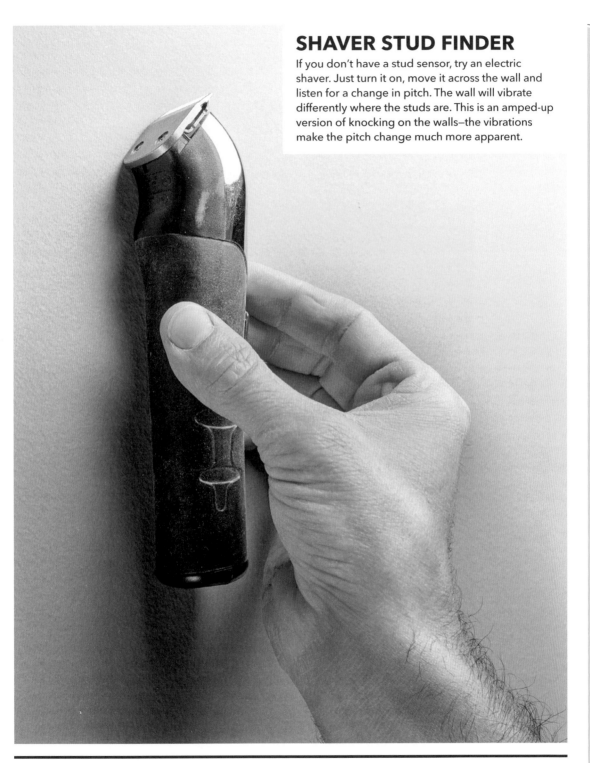

SHAVER STUD FINDER

If you don't have a stud sensor, try an electric shaver. Just turn it on, move it across the wall and listen for a change in pitch. The wall will vibrate differently where the studs are. This is an amped-up version of knocking on the walls—the vibrations make the pitch change much more apparent.

CLEAN OUT THE HOLE

When you drill a hole, dust settles to the bottom and clings to the sides of it. The dust could keep your fastener from embedding all the way or cause a sleeve or wedge to slip. Use a vacuum and a copper fitting brush to remove all the dust.

Copper fitting brush

Smoother Caulk

If you typically cut caulk tube nozzles at an angle to get a nice bead in corners, you've probably noticed a problem when you have to switch direction while caulking: The cut edge is in the wrong place to continue the bead. Instead, cut the nozzle straight and then round it smooth on all sides with an abrasive pad or a nylon carpet scrap. Just rub the cut edge for a minute or so until it's smooth. Now you can caulk in any direction with a nice, continuous bead. Give it a try!

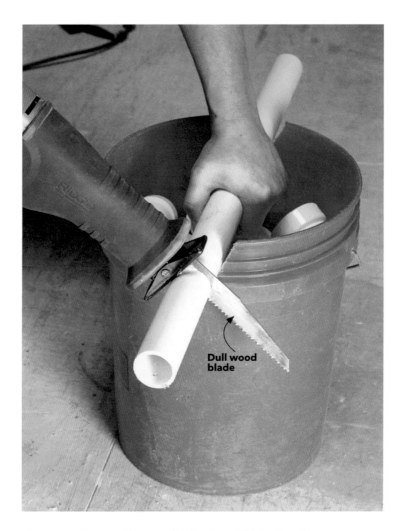

Dull wood blade

Cut Plastic with Dull Blades

In some cases a dull blade is preferable: Cutting plastic pipe with a sharp, aggressive blade can cause the teeth to grab the pipe and jerk it back and forth instead of cutting it. A dull wood blade cuts through plastic almost as well as a blade specifically designed for the task.

CHECK FOR LEAKS

When working on plumbing, do a thorough leak check once everything is connected and your water is back on. Wipe everything down with a dry rag, and then blot your connections with toilet paper to see if you find any evidence of a slow leak.

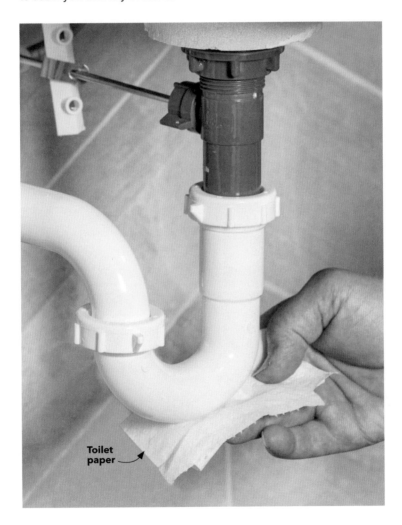

Toilet paper

HIDE OLD HOLES WITH BACK PLATES

If you're switching from a door or cabinet pull to a knob, or you'd prefer to select pulls with a different hole pattern, you can cover the old holes (or hide damaged surfaces) with back plates. Home centers don't have a huge selection, so consider buying yours from an online source such as *myknobs.com*. You'll find hundreds to choose from.

Kitchen Chalk-Up

Before you buy appliances and cabinetry for a new kitchen or a remodel, "try them on" with a mock-up. Use tape, chalk and paper to make a scale drawing on the walls. Also tape the floor to indicate the depths of appliances and cabinets to ensure a good fit.

Get an Extra Hand from Jack

Hanging cabinets solo is slow, frustrating work. A car jack, boosted by scrap wood, can hold a cabinet steady for as long as needed—and without a complaint.

BLOW OUT THE DUST

If drilling dust is left in the hole, it can prevent fasteners from being driven all the way in. You can remove it with a vacuum or blower. But an ear syringe for babies (sold at drugstores) works great and fits nicely in a toolbox. Shove it into the hole and puff out the dust.

Baby ear
syringe

HOW DEEP TO GO

Improvise a depth gauge for measuring blind holes by turning two nuts on a bolt. Place the bolt in a pilot hole and run the nuts down to the surface of the workpiece. Tighten the top nut to hold the measure.

Laminate Flooring Bench Top

Leftover scraps of laminate flooring make a great workbench surface. Laminate is tough and easy to clean—dried glue or paint scrapes right off. If you fasten the laminate with small nails, you can easily pry it off and replace it every few years.

Nonslip Screwdriver

Give your screwdriver a better grip on tough screws by dabbing gritty abrasive on the tip. Valve grinding compound works best, but if you don't want to make a trip to the auto parts store, try this: Add a few drops of water to scouring powder to make a paste, and dip the screwdriver in it.

PREVENT SCRATCHES AND CHIP-OUT

When using a saw, apply tape to the material you're cutting. This accomplishes three things: It prevents the saw's shoe from scuffing your wood, allows you to make an accurate and visible (dark) cutting mark you won't have to sand away, and helps prevent chip-out.

TRACKING BELT SANDER PROGRESS

Draw pencil "progress" lines over the surface while you're belt sanding. As the lines disappear, you'll be able to keep track of which areas have been sanded and where more work is needed.

Progress lines

MICRO-ADJUST A MITER

Close a gap on the top of a miter by placing a skinny shim (1/16 in. or less) against the portion of the fence farthest from the blade. Slide the molding tight to the shim and against the fence near the blade. Hold it in this position while you make the cut. To close a gap at the bottom of the miter, place the shim near the blade. **Caution:** Keep your fingers at least 6 in. from the path of the blade.

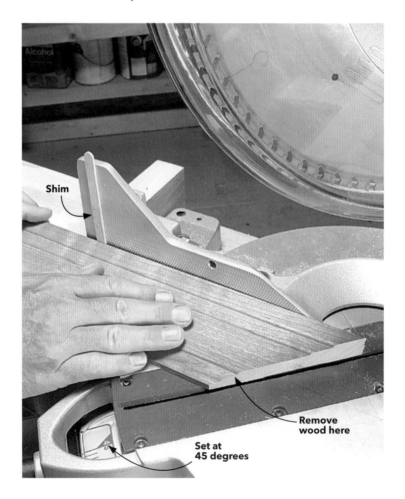

Shim

Remove
wood here

Set at
45 degrees

Rigid foam backer

Cut Plywood on a Foam Backer

Cut full-size sheets of plywood on top of a sheet of 1-in. rigid foam. The foam won't dull the blade, and the cut-off parts won't crash to the floor.

Electric Carving
Knife in the Shop

Have some rigid polyurethane foam, Styrofoam or soft upholstery
foam you want to cut? Smuggle the electric carving knife out of the
kitchen and use that. It works fabulously for any cut you need to make.
Just don't get busted at the border by the kitchen cop! But if you do,
it's safe to say you didn't wreck the knife.

PERFECT MITER JOINTS EVERY TIME

Here's the way to ensure gap-free miter joints when you're edge-banding plywood. Before you cut the trim board miters, tape 45-degree "fitting" boards to the plywood corners. Now you can cut the trim to fit, shaving off a little wood at a time until you reach perfection. Once you've glued on two opposing sides, fit and trim the other two pieces using the glued-on pieces as guides.

Fitting board

REMOVE HARDENED GLUE WITH A PAINT SCRAPER

We've all been there: You glue up your project and then quit for the night. The next day you discover the rock-hard glue and realize that you forgot to scrape off the glue squeeze-out. Don't despair. A sharp paint scraper makes fast work of hardened glue. Either a sharp steel scraper or, better yet, a carbide paint scraper, will pop off all those glue beads in a heartbeat.

Hardened wood glue

Simple Tool Bed Waxing

You can coat a metal table saw and planer bed with auto wax to make the wood slide nicely across the metal. But some expert cabinetmakers use a more convenient product: waxed paper. Keep a roll in your shop drawer and rub a sheet of it over the metal beds on your table saw, router, planer and disc sander. The wax coating doesn't last as long as a good paste wax, but boy, is it a lot easier and quicker to use.

Inject Glue with a Compressor

Ever tried to work glue into a crack with a toothpick? It kind of works, but it's slow and sloppy. A blast of air, on the other hand, drives the glue in deep, evenly and fast. Don't have an air compressor? Hold your shop vacuum nozzle under the crack so it can suck glue deep into the crack.

WHEN PRECISION MATTERS

Different measuring tapes may give you measurements that differ slightly, and sometimes even a 1/16-in. variation spells trouble. So when building furniture, pick one tape, label it and use it throughout the job.

A DRY BRUSH IS HANDY

A brush with no finish on it, or one that's been thoroughly wiped, is a helpful tool. Use it to wipe excess finish out of crevices, which you often find on trim and furniture. You can also use a dry brush for areas that tend to get too much finish, such as edges and corners. It'll pick up the excess finish and prevent sags and drips.

SHARPER CHALK LINES

The fastest way to make straight cutting lines on plywood is to use a chalk line. But before you lay the line on the plywood, give it a quick midair twang. That first twang will get rid of excess chalk, and your mark will be less fuzzy and easier to follow. This is an especially important step to do right after filling your chalk line.

Chalk line

Beat a Bent Blade

When a reciprocating saw blade bends, the obvious fix is to straighten it with pliers or your hammer claw. But that's not the best way; it kinks the blade and never gets it quite straight. Better to think like a blacksmith and hammer it flat. Lay the blade on any nearby wood scrap with the hump facing up. Then pound until it flattens out.

Paint Tray Liner

Glad Press'n Seal plastic wrap (or a similar product) is meant to seal food containers. But it also makes a great paint tray liner. When you're done painting, just peel the sticky plastic off the tray and throw it away—no paint-caked tray to clean up.

FREE PAINT

For your home's exterior and most of the interior, it makes sense to pay for new, high-quality paint. But for closets and utility items such as storage shelves, save money by visiting your city or county recycling center or hazardous waste facility. You may be able to take as much paint as you like—for free. You can also check online marketplaces for your community, as *freecycle.org*.

SOAKER BUCKET

When it comes to watering, slower is better because water soaks in rather than runs off the soil. Slow watering usually means running your garden hose at a trickle or using a soaker hose. Here's a way to soak the soil without dragging hoses around: Drill four 1/8-in. holes in the bottom of a bucket and set it next to thirsty plants.

Gentle-Grip Wheelbarrow Handles

Cut 8-in.-long pieces from an old bicycle tube and pull them over wheelbarrow handles for a solid, comfortable grip during heavy-duty hauling. If the rubber is too stiff to work with, heat it with a hair dryer to soften it.

Cut and Roll Through Posts

Even though the cutting capacity for traditional 7-1/4-in. circular saws is only about 2-1/2 in., you can easily cut through thicker posts. Mark the cut and make the first full-depth cut on one side, then roll the material backward and use the saw kerf to line up the next cut. A third roll and cut will saw through a 4x4 post. If you're working with larger lumber such as 6x6 posts, you'll have to cut on all four sides and finish it off with a handsaw or reciprocating saw.

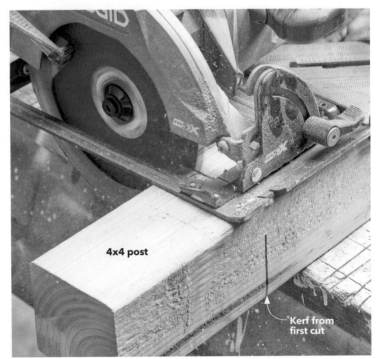

4x4 post

Kerf from first cut

FAST, FLAWLESS VINYL SIDING

VINYL HAS LONG been a popular choice for siding projects, and for good reason: It's inexpensive, it breathes, it doesn't need painting and it's easy to work with. Here are some tips for installing it.

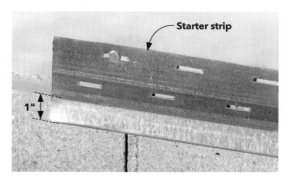

Starter strip

1"

Hide the Seams

On the sides of the house, start each row at the back corner so you don't see the seams from the street. If the seams overlap away from the line of sight, they become nearly invisible. Lap them the other way and they'll be an eyesore.

On the front and back of the house, overlap the seams so you don't see them from the areas where you spend the most time, like front doors, decks and patios. If the visibility of a seam doesn't matter at all, install the siding so the prevailing winds will blow over the seams, not into them.

Use the Wider Starter Strip
The bottom of the starter strip (the part the bottom panel hooks on to) should be at least 1 in. below the top of the foundation, but the lower the siding is installed, the better. It protects the sheathing from rain, snow and pests. Most suppliers sell two sizes of starter, 2-1/2 in. and 3-1/2 in. Spend the extra few bucks on the wider stuff and start your siding a bit lower.

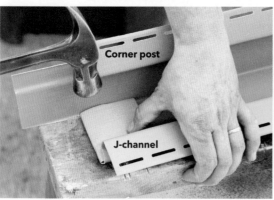

Corner post

J-channel

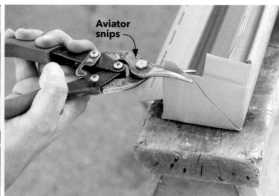

Aviator snips

Cap the Corner Posts
Mice, bees and all sorts of other critters love making their home inside vinyl corner posts. Keep these pests out by capping each post before you install it. Start by cutting off a few inches of the J-channel portion on the post. Fold back the remaining flaps and gently tap a crease into them with your hammer. Notch the flaps so the post will fit snug up against the wall. The posts will crack if they're not warm, so if it's cold outside, place them in the sun or bring them into the house before you do this.

Pull Up As You Nail

Most vinyl siding failures are caused when panels unlock from each other. Once this happens, it's only a matter of time before the wind catches them and sends them flying into the neighbor's yard. Apply a little upward pressure as you nail each piece; this keeps the panels locked together nice and tight. Don't power-lift each piece or you'll put too much pressure on the nailing flange, causing it to break.

Buy a Vinyl Siding Blade

Pushing through vinyl siding with a wood blade in your circular saw will cause the siding to shatter, which is both frustrating and dangerous. Buy a blade made to cut vinyl siding. If you're using a sliding miter saw and the siding is still chipping, try slowly pulling the saw backward through the siding.

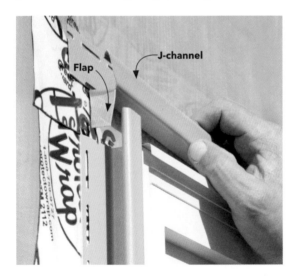

Flap

J-channel

Overlap Your Top J-Channels!

There's no way to stop rainwater from getting into the J-channel that sits on the top of windows and doors. But you can stop that water from getting behind the side J-channels. Create a flap in the top J-channel that overlaps the side channels.

Nailing Fundamentals

- Use 2-in. galvanized roofing nails unless the sheathing has foam on it. In that case, you'll want longer ones.
- Don't drive the nails tight: Each panel should be able to move back and forth or the siding will bubble on really hot days.
- Hit every stud: Expansion and contraction of the siding will loosen nails that are fastened only to the sheathing.

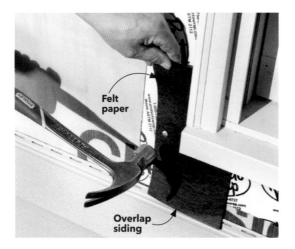

Flash the Bottom of Windows

Cut a piece of flashing out of felt paper and install it at the bottom corners of the windows before you install the side J-channels. Overlap the flashing onto the row of siding just below the window. Now, any water that runs inside the J-channels will come out on top of the siding and out the weep holes designed for this purpose.

Install Longer Panels First

When installing siding around a window or door, start on the side that needs the longer panels. Longer panels don't stretch as readily as smaller ones, so they're not as easy to adjust if they get out of whack. Before nailing the last couple of pieces on the small side, measure up to the top of the window to make sure both sides are at the same height.

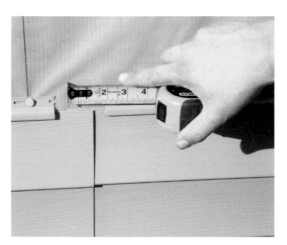

Mind the Overlaps

Always refer to the installation guide on the particular siding that you're installing, but most vinyl siding panels should overlap each other by at least an inch. I add 3/8 in. on hot days because the siding will contract when the temperature drops.

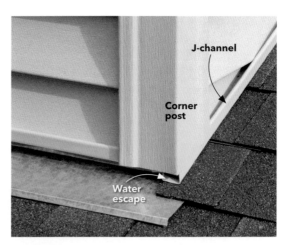

Don't Trap Water Behind Corners

Corner posts above the roofline are a notorious source of water infiltration. If a corner post is installed tight to the shingles and the J-channel dead-ends into it, any water that runs down the J-channel will back up at the post, and may find its way into the house. Instead, hold the corner post up a bit and run the J-channel beneath it.

Install Kick-Out Flashing

Kick-out flashing prevents water from running down a roof and behind the siding on an adjacent wall. It can be a pain to side around it, but you'll fail your inspection if the inspector doesn't see it on your job. Leave the flashing loose and slide the first panel behind it. Then nail the flashing to the wall. Lap the next piece over it. You may need a small trim nail to hold the seam tight (a little dab of caulk over the trim nail is a good idea).

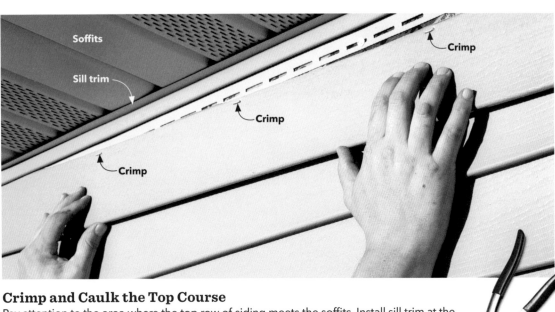

Crimp and Caulk the Top Course

Pay attention to the area where the top row of siding meets the soffits. Install sill trim at the soffits, rip down the top course of siding and crimp the siding so the sill trim holds it in place. Add a few blobs of caulk inside the bottom lip of the top course for extra security. You can crimp the siding using a Malco Snap Lock Punch or a similar tool.

TEST YOUR DIY IQ!

OK, Einstein, you think you're one smart handyman?

TAKE OUR DIY IQ TEST to find out! Here's how it works:

1. Easy, intermediate and really tough questions are all mixed together.

2. A question may have more than one correct answer.

3. You'll find the answers on p. 222-223. Good luck!

1 The actual width of a 2x12 is:

A. 11-1/2 in.
B. 11 in.
C. 11-1/4 in.
D. 12 in.

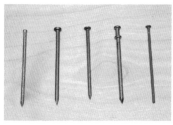

2 Your project calls for size 16d nails. What does "d" stand for?

A. Penny
B. Diameter
C. Decimeter
D. Denarius

3 Which type of plastic pipe requires a primer before it can be cemented?

A. PVC
B. ABS
C. Plastic conduit
D. All of the above

4 Which type of "ell" is the elbow shown?

A. Short sweep
B. Long sweep
C. Tennis
D. Vent

5 What's the main difference between mortar and concrete?

A. No difference; they're both names for the same material.
B. Mortar contains bonding agents; concrete does not.
C. Concrete has gravel added; mortar has only sand.
D. Mortar is made from Portland cement. Concrete is made from conventional cement.

6 Let's say you would like to pour a concrete slab that's 11 ft. x 16 ft. and 4 in. thick. How much concrete would it take to fill the forms?

A. 3.5 yards
B. 4 yards
C. 1.25 yards
D. 2.2 yards

7 True or False: This method of fastening is called pocket screw joinery.

8 True or False: This is a "flush trim" router bit.

9 You have two pieces of wood that need to be glued together. However, there are gaps as large as 1/16 in. between the boards. The best type of glue to use is:

A. Polyurethane
B. Wood glue thickened with sawdust
C. Epoxy
D. Superglue

10 If your garbage disposer hums but won't spin, what should you check?

A. The kitchen GFCI
B. The reset button on the underside of the disposer
C. The water supply
D. The disposer to see if something is lodged inside

C. If your ears aren't ringing, there's no permanent damage.
D. Damaged hearing will improve if you begin wearing hearing protection.

15 When you wire a receptacle, you should ...
A. Put the hot (black or red) wire under the brass screw.
B. Put the neutral (white) wire under the brass screw.
C. Either (A) or (B); the outlet will work either way.
D. Neither (A) nor (B); use the stab-in connectors on the back.

Galvanic corrosion

16 You're installing a new water heater and are faced with joining galvanized piping and copper tubing. What connector should you use to prevent galvanic corrosion?
A. Threaded plastic nipple
B. Dielectric coupling
C. Copper (threaded or sweat) coupling
D. Dielectric nipple

17 A double-headed (duplex) nail is used for what purpose?
A. Bracing temporary walls
B. Fastening concrete forms
C. Attaching plywood patches over blown-out or missing windows and doors
D. All of the above

11 What's the proper term for this outlet?
A. AFCI
B. GFIF
C. GFCI
D. FDCI

12 What is the most common spacing used for wall studs and floor joists?
A. 16 in.
B. 19-3/16 in.
C. 24 in.
D. 12 in.

13 What is the biggest cause of house fires?
A. Unattended cooking
B. Electrical shorts
C. Open flames (candles, etc.)
D. Children playing with lighters and matches

14 Which of the following statements is true?
A. When you are subjected to noise above 85 decibels, you experience permanent hearing loss.
B. Because of its high pitch, a belt sander poses a particular risk to your hearing.

18 What type of cut is this guy making?
A. Dado
B. Rabbet
C. Groove
D. Miter

19 You should fill your car tires to what pressure?
A. The maximum tire pressure listed on the sidewall of the tire to give you the best possible gas mileage.
B. A good rule of thumb is 10 lbs. under the maximum pressure.
C. It depends entirely on driving conditions.
D. The pressure recommended on the driver's-side doorpost

20 Which building product is often referred to by its brand name, "Romex"?
A. Electrical cable
B. PVC piping
C. Drywall
D. Vinyl siding

DIY IQ Answers

1 **(C)**. A 2x12 is typically 11-1/4 in. wide. A 2x4 is 3-1/2 in. wide and a 2x6 is 5-1/2 in. wide. On sizes larger than that, all dimensional lumber drops to the next 1/4-in. increment. A 2x8 is 7-1/4 in. wide and a 2x10 is 9-1/4 in. wide.

NAIL SIZES DECODED

SIZE	LENGTH
4d	1-1/2"
6d	2"
8d	2-1/2"
10d	3"
12d	3-1/4"
16d	3-1/2"
20d	4"

(There is some variation.)

2 **(A)** and **(D)**. It stands for penny and also denarius (hence the "d"). In Roman times there was a small coin called the denarius, and the abbreviation "d" became associated with pennies. Centuries ago, when nails were made by hand, they were priced by how many pennies it took to buy 100 nails. So for a longish nail, 16 pennies (d) would buy 100 nails. The system evolved so that 16d refers just to the length of the nail. The chart shows you what each penny designation means in inches.

3 **(A)**. Only PVC needs primer. It softens the outer surface with a more concentrated solvent than is used in the cement.

4 **(D)**. Vent elbow. Vent elbows have the sharpest bend, because they carry only air, never liquid. Short sweep and long sweep elbows are for liquid, so they have wider bends. Here's a rule of thumb for knowing whether to use a long or a short sweep. If water is speeding up as it turns the corner (usually going from horizontal to vertical), use a short sweep. If water is slowing down (usually from vertical to horizontal), use a long sweep.

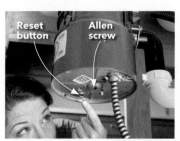
Long sweep / Short sweep / Vent

5 **(C)**. Concrete has sand and gravel; mortar has only sand. In both cases, the sand and gravel ("aggregate") are added to the cement to form a matrix, greatly increasing its strength.

6 **(D)**. The correct answer is 2.2 yards, but it's very smart to order an extra quarter yard to make sure you have enough. Here's how the calculation works. Multiply .33 (one-third of a foot, or 4 in.) x 11 x 16 to get 58 cubic feet. Since there's 27 cubic feet in 1 cubic yard, you just divide 58 by 27 and get 2.15 yards. Rounded up, that's 2.2 yards.

7 True.

8 False. A flush trim bit has the bearing below the cutters. The bit shown is called a pattern bit. It's used to follow an existing edge to cut a matching one on a board below. That's why the bearing is above the cutters.

9 **(C)**. Epoxy is the strongest gap-filling glue. It will not only stick to the surfaces but also fill gaps. Polyurethane, wood glue and cyanoacrylate (that is, super glue) need surfaces in close proximity for a strong bond.

Reset button / Allen screw

10 **(D)**. Check for blockage. Make sure the power is off, then put your hand in and remove the offending object or material. Celery fibers and potato peels can stop the motor, but you may not be able to pull them free. That's when you grab an Allen wrench and manually turn the motor to free the cutters. Once it's turning, you may have to push the reset button on the underside of the disposer (see above) to reset the internal breaker.

11 **(C)**. GFCI, which stands for ground fault circuit interrupter. If it senses that some current is going to a ground (if you dropped an electric razor in a sink full of water, for example), the GFCI shuts off the circuit in a fraction of a second to protect you from an electrical shock.

12 **(A).** Framing is most commonly spaced every 16 in., but all four listed spacings are used.

13 **(A).** Unattended cooking, by far. In fact, 23% of home fires start on stovetops. Hot grease or oil ignites and in turn ignites anything combustible nearby. A common scenario is someone carrying a flaming frying pan outside and dripping flaming grease on the carpet and furniture on the way out, starting a much larger fire. You should cover pans that are aflame with a lid to smother the fire. By the way, smoking in bed claims the title for the most fatalities.

14 **(A).** Permanent hearing damage starts at 85dB. Belt sanders are among the quietest power tools, although they are still above the 85dB threshold. Many other power tools exceed that threshold, including shop vacuums. Hammer drills can be louder than 115dB. And once you lose some of your hearing, it's gone forever.

15 **(A).** The hot wire(s) should go under the brass screw(s). The neutral wire(s), which are almost always white, should go under the silver screw. Remember: Silver = white.

The outlet will still work if you do it backward, but many devices you're plugging into it won't be safe. For example, you may be energizing the outside metal parts of a lamp, creating a shock hazard. Stab-in connectors are notoriously unreliable unless they have a setscrew. Then they're fine.

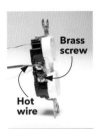

Brass screw

Hot wire

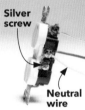

Silver screw

Neutral wire

16 **(D).** Dielectric nipple. Whenever you join copper water lines to galvanized steel pipe, you should be concerned about the corrosion caused by joining two dissimilar metals, called galvanic corrosion. An electrochemical reaction occurs that causes the steel pipe to rust and clog up. Short dielectric couplings have a short plastic nipple to keep the metals from touching, but the metals are still close enough to cause a reaction and corrosion. The better solution is to use a longer fitting called a dielectric nipple. A 3-in.-long plastic liner inside the fitting keeps the metals apart to greatly reduce corrosion.

Dielectric nipple

17 **(D).** Double-headed (duplex) nails are used to temporarily attach any wood parts together. The top head protrudes above the wood, making it easy to pull it out when needed.

18 **(C).** A groove is a slot that goes with the grain. A rabbet is simply a square notch at the edge of plywood or lumber. A dado is a slot that goes across the grain, used mostly to anchor permanent shelves.

19 **(D).** Use the pressure listed on the doorpost. The proper pressure is carefully figured out by

the car manufacturers, taking into account weight, weight distribution and the handling characteristics for each car model. Maximum pressure is just that. It's the most pressure the tire can handle safely. It is rarely the pressure you should use.

20 **(A).** Romex is one of the leading brands of NM (nonmetallic sheathed) electrical cable, used for most residential home wiring. The name is derived from the original manufacturer's name: the Rome Cable Company, based in Rome, NY.